D1292670

Lake Erie
Walleye

By Mark Hicks

Frank A. Scalish

Big River Press

Introduction

FOR MORE THAN a decade, Lake Erie has easily reigned as the world's greatest walleye fishery. Other bodies of water simply can't compete. Anglers who venture here from regions that claim to be walleye strongholds are stunned by the size and number of walleyes they catch from Lake Erie.

Today's Lake Erie, with its clear water and splendid fishing, is the result of a dramatic transformation. When I attended high school in the Cleveland area in the late 60s, pollution suffocated Lake Erie's walleye and unregulated commercial netting grasped them in a stranglehold. Walleye stocks plummeted to all-time lows.

Thanks to anti-pollution measures, commercial netting regulations and other factors, Lake Erie's water quality has steadily improved and its walleyes have rebounded.

Anglers have enjoyed extraordinary fishing here, but lately the walleyes have grown more elusive. The cause is the zebra mussel, which invaded the Great Lakes in the late 80s. This tiny, nonindigenous shellfish has thrived. It so efficiently filters plankton from the water that Lake Erie has grown markedly clearer.

Walleyes are adjusting to the increased water clarity by changing their habits. They now feed more at night and have become notably boat shy during the day. Catching walleyes from Lake Erie today requires anglers to alter their fishing strategies. That's where this book can help.

The following pages explain how Lake Erie walleye are responding to continuing environmental changes. In addition, the book reveals the latest and most productive Lake Erie fishing methods used by eminent charter captains and the nation's top professional walleye anglers.

Lake Erie will continue producing great walleye fishing in the years ahead. This book will help you take advantage of this exciting fishery.

Mark Hicks

Acknowledgements

Writing a book on Lake Erie walleye fishing is an imposing task. This is a big subject. Doing it justice has required a considerable effort and a great deal of help. Over the course of several months I interviewed biologists, charter captains and expert anglers who provided invaluable information on how and where to catch walleyes throughout Lake Erie.

At the outset, I met with Fred Snyder from Ohio Sea Grant and tapped his vast warehouse of knowledge. Sea Grant specialists Dave Kelch and Frank Lichtkoppler also provided valuable insights.

I also interviewed fisheries biologists scattered all around Lake Erie, including Roger Knight and Kevin Kayle from Ohio, Bob Haas and Bill McClay from Michigan, Don Einhouse from New York state, Roger Kenyon from Pennsylvania, and Bryan Henderson, Les Sztramko, Steve Nepszy and Dr. Joe Leach from Ontario.

A long list of charter captains, professional walleye anglers and fishing experts graciously passed along priceless information about how and where to catch walleyes from Lake Erie. They include Capt. Eddy Able, Capt. Pete Alex, Capt. Joe Belanger, Mark Brumbaugh, Capt. Pat Chrysler, Joe DeBuysser, Capt. Dave Demeter, Capt. Dave Demeter Jr., Capt. Andy Emrisko, Capt. Jim Fofrich, Capt. Art Grayling, Capt. Ron Johnson, Keith Kavajecz, Capt. Bill King, Rick LaCourse, Capt. Jerry Lee, Capt. Al Lesh, Art Lyons, Ted Malota, Mike McClelland, Gary Parsons, Gary Roach, Scott Stecher, Jim Stedke, Ted Takasaki, Capt. Dean Thompson, Capt. Bob Troxel and Capt. Phil Whitt.

Also thanks to Bill Hilts, promotion coordinator of Niagara County Sportfishing in New York state and Bob Chandler of the Erie Convention Bureau in Pennsylvania.

Mitch Cox and Bill Sedivy deserve my gratitude for helping with their sharp editor's pencils.

Lake Erie Walleye
Copyright 1996 Big River Press

Printed in the U.S.A.

ISBN 0-9643309-1-1

Contents

Section One: Lake Erie Fishing Tactics

Section Two: Seasonal Walleye Movements

Cover Photograph: Mike McClelland poses with a Lake Erie walleye in front of Perry's Monument on South Bass Island.

Dedication

To Mom and Dad, who taught me how to fish and to appreciate the outdoors.

Chapter 1

The Richest Sweetwater Sea

Part of the largest freshwater system on earth, Lake Erie forms the southernmost link in the chain of the Great Lakes. It is the second smallest of these five sweetwater seas, yet Lake Erie yields more pounds of fish for human consumption than all the other Great Lakes combined. It may be the most productive freshwater fishery the world has ever seen.

Today, Lake Erie's vast walleye population commands attention from sport anglers nationwide. Recent professional tournaments here have set records that make other walleye waters pale by comparison. During one major event in 1993, the *average* weight of more than 2,000 walleyes checked in was just under 7.3 pounds!

The walleye is only one of over 130 species of fish that have been discovered in Lake Erie, including the thriving smallmouth bass. Some of this richness stems from the fact that Lake Erie is the shallowest of the Great Lakes, with an average depth of just 62 feet. Compare that to an average depth of 500 feet for Lake Superior, 279 for Lake Michigan, 194 for Lake Huron and 282 for Lake Ontario.

Lake Erie's shallow nature and southerly location warms the water that flows into its west end from Lake Huron through Lake St. Clair and the Detroit River. The Maumee, Sandusky and other major Ohio rivers also supply water and nutrients. The warm, fertile water stimulates the growth of microorganisms that comprise food for bait fish and other organisms. They, in turn, provide abundant forage for species up the food chain, including the walleye.

THREE BASINS OF LAKE ERIE

As we know it today, Lake Erie has existed for only about 2,000 years, roughly since the birth of Christ. Stretching 210 miles northeast from Toledo, Ohio, to Buffalo, New York—with a breadth of 57 miles—it contains three distinctly different sections, called basins.

The western basin lies west of an imaginary line extending across the lake from Cedar Point, Ohio, to Pelee Point, Ontario. While smaller and shallower than the other basins, it forms the nucleus for the world's greatest walleye fishery.

Averaging only 24 feet deep, the western basin contains spacious, hard-bottom reefs that furnish ideal spawning habitat for millions of walleyes every spring. Add to this the Maumee and Sandusky rivers, which both support spawning runs of walleyes. Walleyes also spawn near shorelines on sandy bottoms east and north of Toledo, Ohio.

The western basin warms weeks ahead of the rest of the lake, allowing walleyes to commence spawning earlier in the spring. Joint tagging studies conducted by Ohio, Michigan, Ontario, Pennsylvania and New York indicate that the vast majority of walleyes in Lake Erie migrate to the western basin to spawn. This includes walleyes that comprise the bulk of the fishery in the central and eastern basins during the summer months,

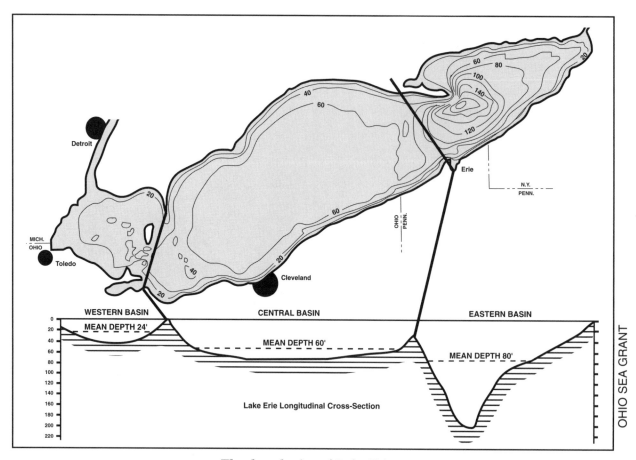

The three basins of Lake Erie.

and even fish that migrate down from Lake Huron, through Lake St. Clair and the Detroit River.

The central basin stretches from Cedar Point, Ohio, to Erie, Pennsylvania, and claims the distinction of being the largest section of the lake. In the western basin, Lake Erie laps against flat lands that were once marshes. Water in the clearer, deeper central basin, however, washes against cliffs.

The bottom drops off more sharply in the central basin, with depths to 30 feet often within a mile of shore. The middle of the central basin dips to more than 80 feet deep, but the bottom in most areas remains flat and featureless.

Walleye fishing in the central basin doesn't get into full swing until the fish move east from the western basin after spawning. Some walleyes do spawn on rocky bottoms near shore, but this type of habitat is limited.

The eastern basin, stretching from Erie Pennsylvania, to Buffalo, New York, is the deepest and clearest portion of Lake Erie. It is bordered by cliffs, features deeper water near shore and plunges to a depth of 210 feet. In this basin, near shore walleye spawning does occur. But, as with the central basin, it is the influx of walleyes from the west that sustains the optimum summertime fishing.

The variety of habitat furnished by Lake Erie's three basins contributes to its ability to support large and diverse fish populations. The lake's fast "flushing time" also helps. While decades must pass before the other Great Lakes replace their water, Lake Erie flows through in only about three years. Lake Superior, in contrast, has a retention time of well over 100 years.

Were it not for this fast flushing time, Lake Erie now would be little more than an open sewer.

HISTORICAL PERSPECTIVE

When European explorers ventured into the North American continent, they followed waterways that had been navigated for centuries by native Indians. This provided a faster route to the interior than traveling over country that had yet to taste the settler's ax.

After negotiating Ontario's Ottawa and Mattawa Rivers to Lake Nipissing, explorers took the French River to Georgian Bay, which joins with Lake Huron. Because of its southern location, Lake Erie was the last of the Great Lakes to be discovered. Most historians believe Louis Joliet was the first white man to see Lake Erie. He did so in 1669 thanks to an Iroquois guide who brought him from Lake Superior, down through Lake Erie, while en route back to Montreal.

OHIO SEA GRANT

Perry's Monument on South Bass Island.

Before settlement, the banks and the country around Lake Erie supported thick hardwood forests that had stood virtually untouched by humans. Seemingly endless stands of beech and maple predominated, but there also were forests of oak and hickory, and oak mixed with conifers. On the western end of the lake, elm and ash trees grew tall in the impenetrable Great Black Swamp, which covered 1,500 square miles.

Clear water filtered into the western basin through wetlands that were thick with wild rice and other aquatic growth, especially at the mouths of the Ottawa, Maumee and Portage rivers. More than 300 species of birds found these wetlands to their liking, including bald eagles, geese, ducks, herons, egrets and gulls.

Lake Erie's clear water, untainted by pollution, was sweet to the taste and supported strong populations of predatory fish, including walleye, blue pike, sauger, smallmouth bass, pike, muskellunge and lake trout. Some of the other prominent species included yellow perch, white bass, whitefish, several kinds of herring, sturgeon, cisco and channel catfish. There were no carp, white perch, brown trout, rainbow trout, alewives, or Pacific salmon. These species were later introduced by man.

Fish from Lake Erie provided sustenance for the earliest Europeans who ventured into the region. During spring spawning runs up rivers, many species could easily be seen in the clear water. At times they were so thick that a blind stab with a spear would impale a fish more often than not. Wild game also provided essential food.

The rich fur trade lured Europeans into this territory during the latter part of the 17th century.

Trading posts on the Cuyahoga, Sandusky and Maumee rivers made Lake Erie an important part of this early economy.

Initially, the French and British managed to share the country with few problems, mainly because the French practically monopolized the interior. But as the British grew more intrusive, conflicts erupted that continued for more than 100 years.

Because it was such a critical trade route, Lake Erie witnessed countless battles, especially at forts Niagara and Detroit, which controlled the navigable rivers leading to the other Great Lakes. These often ruthless, bloody encounters frequently employed Indians. While the French enjoyed more success wooing Indians to their causes, there were occasions when certain tribes sided with the British.

During and after the American Revolution, Indians—often supplied with weapons from the British—fought Americans to retain possession of their domain. The mighty Iroquois, who had reigned over the lands of eastern Lake Erie for 200 years, were the last major threat to settlers. The league fell from power in 1779 when its villages and crops in western New York were destroyed by a U.S. Army.

The withdrawal of British troops from Erie's south shore in 1796 opened the door for settlement. There would be subsequent Indian wars and treaties, but an unstoppable wave of white Europeans now flooded into this untamed tract.

In the War of 1812, the final U.S. military clash with Britain, both sides struggled for control of Lake Erie because it afforded an easy avenue of attack. The high point of the war took place when six British ships, their entire Lake Erie fleet, sailed into the waters northwest of South Bass Island.

Oliver Hazard Perry, commanding a U.S. fleet of nine vessels, subdued the intruders in a blazing, 3-hour duel. The battle was the turning point that eventually lead the U.S. to victory. Today, Perry's Monument on South Bass Island stands as an historical tribute to this event and serves as an unmistakable landmark for walleye fishermen.

PARADISE LOST

Up to this point, man had imposed little impact on Lake Erie and its fish populations. Changes followed rapidly, however, as settlers flocked into the region. They viewed the dense forest as an enemy, something to be dreaded, conquered and put to use.

9

Shipping made the shores of Lake Erie an ideal location for industry.

Virgin woodlands toppled and the rich soil immediately felt the steel of the farmer's plow. The resources in this vast land seemed limitless. No one gave a thought to preservation.

By 1890, practically every stand of virgin timber in the Lake Erie basin had been felled. Even today, forests cover only about 10 percent of the land. Swamp lands and marshes were drained, deforested and converted to crop lands, including the Great Black Swamp.

The erosion of soils from crop lands muddied the rivers, spoiled spawning areas for fish, hindered aquatic growth and poured sediments into Lake Erie. By 1900, the rooted aquatic vegetation that had once formed lush meadows in Maumee and Sandusky bays was nearly gone.

Farmers could do little with the grain they harvested until it had been ground into flour. By 1820, mill dams sprung up on nearly every Lake Erie tributary that was capable of powering these simple machines. Today, mill dams may appear quaint, harmless and picturesque, but they effectively blocked the upstream spawning runs of dozens of fish. Sturgeon, pike, muskellunge and other species have never recovered from that devastating blow.

The development of transportation systems during the mid-1800s transformed Lake Erie into a hub for the industrial revolution. First came an inland canal system (including the famous Erie Canal), then railroads, plus an expanding shipping industry that allowed for the mass movement of goods and raw materials to and from Lake Erie ports.

Immense deposits of iron ore along Lake Superior to the north and vast quantities of coal and oil from Pennsylvania made the shores of Lake Erie an ideal location to cheaply receive the raw materials of industry.

During the 1860s, the Standard Oil Company initiated Cleveland's role as the world's leading oil refinery. At this time coal was replacing wood as a fuel source, and black smoke began pouring from the stacks of Cleveland's iron foundries.

In the western end of the lake, on the banks of the Maumee River, Toledo ranked second to Cleveland in the oil refining industry by the late 1800s. Just after the turn of the century, the Libby Company made Toledo a world leader in the production of glass.

And just up the Detroit River, of course, Henry Ford began mass producing automobiles. Detroit became the Motor City, and Toledo, Sandusky, Cleveland and other Lake Erie communities became crucial suppliers to the burgeoning auto industry.

The growth of industry and agriculture brought a rapidly expanding human population to the shores of Lake Erie. This drastically increased the raw sewage that poured into the rivers and streams entering the lake and directly into the lake itself. This foul matter mixed with industrial pollution and agricultural run-off that washed in chemicals and fertilizers.

The worst of the contamination occurred from about 1930 to the early 70s during the peak of the industrial period. Elliot Tramer, professor of biology at the University of Toledo, describes this period in the book, "The Great Lake Erie."

"In the mid-1950s," he writes, "the cumulative effects of a century and a half of indifference became too obvious to ignore. Water quality investigations revealed an alarming spread of anoxic (deoxygenated) waters, especially in the lake's central basin. Bearing the accelerating costs of harbor dredging and sewage treatment had become a burdensome necessity for taxpayers. Nuisance blue-green algae growths caused by overfertilizing of the lake encumbered boating, fouled beaches and tainted drinking water with their toxins. Excessive bacterial counts closed beaches to swimming, and the spectacular collapse of the commercial fisheries for pike, cisco, lake whitefish and sauger made headlines."

During this period, pollution caused severe oxygen depletion in the lower layers of Lake Erie. Mayflies once rose from the bottom of the western basin in massive hatches, affording a substantial food source for walleyes. They vanished in one season, when anoxia suffocated them before the nymphs could emerge. Several species of bottom dwelling fish also nearly disappeared due to a lack of oxygen, including the burbot, silver chub and mooneye.

When an oil slick on the Cuyahoga River caught fire in the late '60s, it alarmed the nation. Lake Erie was dying. It had become a disgraceful symbol for the consequences of rampant pollution.

UNREGULATED COMMERCIAL FISHING

That walleyes somehow endured the onslaught of pollution is remarkable. But what brought them to the very brink of extermination was commercial netting.

FISH CONSUMPTION ADVISORIES

In 1994 the Ohio departments of health and natural resources released a fish consumption advisory for Lake Erie. It has given some people the notion that new or increased contaminants have been found in fish flesh.

The fact is, the trace amounts of toxins found in Lake Erie fish continue to decline every year. The new advisory stems from a more conservative system of looking at fish contaminants and their potential effects on human health.

In regard to Lake Erie perch and walleye, few anglers will need to reduce the number of fish they eat. Perch have no restrictions and the advisory recommends limiting walleye to one meal a week, or 52 meals per year. Few people eat fish more than 52 times a year.

The commercial fishing industry on Lake Erie got underway in the early 1800s, but it didn't begin taking a substantial toll until the latter part of that century when gill and pound nets were being set throughout the lake. From then on, Lake Erie's most desirable fish quickly declined.

From 1893 to 1900, the commercial catch of walleyes dropped from 13 million pounds to 2 million. Other prominent species also suffered.

H.F. Moore, in his 1894, "Report Upon the Condition and Regulation of the Fisheries of Lake Erie," made the following observations:

"The white fish is the more prized fish of Lake Erie and was at one time the chief object of the fishery. The species was unequal to the demands made upon it and decreased so rapidly that it was supplanted by the herring (cisco)."

Moore noted that walleye and blue pike also were highly regarded. (Closely related to the walleye, the blue pike was smaller, but every bit as succulent.) Yellow perch, however, were held in disdain. When a commercial fisherman told Moore that he had found cisco eggs in the stomachs of perch, Moore didn't mince words:

"Such evidence as this should place this species (yellow perch) entirely beyond the pale of protection. The fisheries would probably be benefited if the perch in Lake Erie were exterminated."

Moore's venom may seem humorous in light of the high esteem in which yellow perch are held as table fare today. But even then, before the end of the 19th century, he was troubled by the senseless disregard for Erie and its waning fisheries. He wrote:

"...all, or nearly all, species that are of commercial importance have undergone heavy decrease and in some cases, as compared with their former abundance, they have been practically expunged from consideration as factors of commercial interest.

"The fisheries of Lake Erie have been too long neglected and shamefully abused.

"The time has now come when a check should be put upon the wasteful methods now pursued not only for the benefit of the fishermen, but that this great reserve of cheap and nutritious food may be saved from utter exhaustion."

Moore's pleas were drowned by the forces of economics, pure greed and a lack of good common sense. Commercial netting continued unabated, as did unregulated sport fishing, to the detriment of Lake Erie and its walleyes.

From the onset of commercial fishing on Erie, when one species of fish decreased, another filled the void and grew more abundant. Netters, undaunted by the absence of their preferred catch, simply shifted their efforts to the next available fish on the priority list. One by one, the most desirable species were either netted to oblivion or to the point that their stocks became badly depleted.

Whitefish, cisco, sturgeon and sauger were soon supplanted by blue pike, yellow perch, walleye, fresh-water drum and carp. Despite pollution and netting, the blue pike sustained an annual harvest of typically more than 10 million pounds until the 1940s. Even more surprising, walleye and blue pike increased significantly during the early 1950s. Sport fishing was good, and the market price for these species plum-meted. No one could have predicted the sudden popu-lation crash of 1957. Only the year before, netters had gathered more than 35 mil-lion pounds of blue pike and walleye. By 1960 blue pike were extinct and the wall-eye harvest dipped to less than 3 million pounds.

Yellow perch soared as they supplanted the blue pike and walleye. It had taken 150 years, but the combined effects of pollu-tion and overharvesting had bankrupted Lake Erie's once exquisite fishery. Yel-low perch dominated as the top food fish, followed by white bass, catfish, carp, freshwater drum and smelt.

Erie's walleye responded quickly to cleaner water and sensible harvest regulations.

ON THE REBOUND

If pollution and commercial netting had contin-ued unchecked, you would not be reading this book because there would be no walleyes in Lake Erie to write about. Fortunately, a combination of events fueled a startling turnabout.

In 1970, one of the first positive developments came in the form of dire news. Ontario had discovered levels of mercury in the flesh of Lake Erie walleye that were too high for safe human consumption. An immediate moratorium on sport and commercial fish-ing for walleyes ensued, giving the remaining fish a stay of execution. During the ban, Ontario and the U.S. states bordering Lake Erie formed an interna-tional management plan that would determine sen-sible harvest limits for fish in the future.

When mercury contamination declined a few years later, sport fishing for walleyes opened through-out Lake Erie. Only Ontario and Pennsylvania still permit commercial walleye fishing, and it appears that Pennsylvania will soon stop.

Ohio, Michigan and New York have ended com-mercial walleye fishing operations. Legislators in these states correctly reasoned that a strong Lake Erie sport fishery would inject hundreds of million of dollars into their economies.

Overdue anti-pollution regulations also spurred the walleye revival. The nation finally realized that an environment too despoiled to support other life forms would eventually turn on the human race. The Clean Water Act of 1972 was one of many crucial pieces of legislation that put Lake Erie, and the country, on the long road to recovery.

Phosphate pollution has steadily declined in re-sponse to improved sewage treatment plants and a re-duction of phosphates in laundry detergents. The battle against toxic pollu-tion from industrial dis-charges and other sources has brought about measur-able improvements in wa-ter quality, as well. Sedi-ments, fertilizers and chemi-cals that wash into the lake with farm run-off continue to be reduced thanks, in part, to the spread of no-till farm-ing practices.

A slowdown in the region's industrial produc-tion also cut back the amount of pollutants entering the lake. An increase in the water level of the Great Lakes provided another windfall for Lake Erie and its walleyes. The addi-tional water diluted pollution and helped flush it out of the system.

By the 1970s, unsightly mats of blue-green algae no longer covered the western and central basins. As the water cleared and became more oxygenated, record walleye hatches launched a booming popula-tion growth. It peaked in the mid-1980s when the estimated population exceeded 120 million walleyes!

During that period, Lake Erie may have harbored more walleyes than at any time in its existence. This was partially due to an imbalance caused by an absence of competitive species. Fisheries biologists worried that the lake would exceed its carrying capac-ity. Daily sport fish limits increased and the Canadian commercial harvest expanded.

Anglers from all over the country swarmed Lake Erie, the newly crowned "Walleye Capital of the

Al Lesh, a Michigan walleye angler, scoops up zebra mussel shells that wash up on Erie's shores by the millions.

lake and compete with native species. Biologists presume that zebra mussels from Europe invaded Lake St. Clair sometime in 1985 or '86, possibly when an ocean freighter dumped ballast water that it had carried from overseas. The tiny, striped mollusks look harmless, but they quickly and dramatically altered the Great Lakes, especially Lake Erie.

Unlike any other freshwater mollusk, zebra mussels have the ability to cling to hard surfaces, including rocky lake bottoms, piers, water intakes and boat hulls. They also reproduce at an astonishing rate. Since their discovery in Lake St. Clair in 1988, zebras have spread throughout the Great Lakes and into some inland waters.

Nowhere have they prospered more than in the shallow, nutrient-rich water of Lake Erie's western basin, where they now thickly encrust the rocky reefs on which walleyes spawn.

"Our greatest concern initially," said District Sea Grant Specialist Fred Snyder, "was that waste material from the zebra mussels would collect on the reefs, making an environment where walleye eggs couldn't incubate.

"But the lake provides enough current to flush out the shell beds. The success of recent spawning seasons has been very good. We've had excellent hatches."

Another concern arises from the zebra's feeding habits. Each mussel filters over a liter of water per day, removing nearly all small particles, including phytoplankton, the base of the food chain. With zebra mussels removing significant amounts of phytoplankton, will Lake Erie support enough forage fish to sustain its monumental walleye population?

Thus far, the forage base remains strong. Some biologists, however, still worry that zebra mussels may undermine the food chain in the future and adversely affect walleyes and other game fish. There has been talk of fertilizing the lake with nutrients should this occur.

One impact of the zebra invasion has been clearly evident, particularly in the western basin. With billions of mussels filtering the water, Erie exhibits an 85-percent increase in water clarity. In areas where 4 feet of visibility was considered clear in the past, it is now common to see bottom 10 to 20 feet deep. The

World." To accommodate them, the charter fishing industry increased from a handful of boats to more than a thousand. Enormous flotillas of fishing boats blanketed the western basin on every weekend. Limit catches became so commonplace that they were expected.

EASY FISHING

Although Erie's water clarity had improved, the western basin was still murky compared to other walleye lakes. The nutrients that clouded the water provided ample nourishment for bait fish, which sustained the walleyes. The dingy water also blocked sunlight penetration and allowed walleyes to feed comfortably throughout the day.

It added up to easy pickings for anglers. You could sleep in, fish through midday, fling weight-forward spinners from a drifting boat and later complain about how many walleyes you had to clean. When anglers discovered walleyes in the clearer central and eastern basins, deep-water trolling methods were employed to dredge them from the depths.

Other fish also profited from the improved water quality. Most native species still exist, though many in limited numbers. Smallmouth bass thrive and other desirable species may again grow prominent.

ZEBRA MUSSEL INVASION

One possible obstacle to these recovering fisheries comes in the form of exotic species that enter the central and eastern basins have always been clearer than the western basin, but, they too, now display even greater water clarity.

Faced with increased light penetration, Erie's walleye feed more at night and during low light periods early and late in the day. In short, they display habits typical of walleyes practically everywhere else. Daytime fishing still produces, but not as consistently as in the past, when murky water prevailed. This is especially true in the western basin.

Walleye also head deeper under sunlit conditions than in the past, and they have grown more boat shy. Occasionally, they still feed carelessly near the surface while a fleet of fishermen drift overhead. But they usually shy from boats, scooting away or swim-

ming deeper to avoid them. An entire school often moves away in response excessive fishing pressure.

Haphazard fishing methods that once produced easy limits of western basin walleye don't cut it today. Even though the walleye population remains stable, the sport fishing catch has dropped. Anglers mired in old methods suffer the most. Consistent fishing success in the clearer water requires more thought, dedication and versatility. Weight-forward spinners and jigs still have their times, but trolling and bottom bouncing rigs have become more commonplace.

Trolling has produced exceptional catches of Lake Erie walleye for Wisconsin angler Gary Parsons, one of the nation's most accomplished walleye pros. Having fished the top walleye waters across the country for several years, he expresses strong opinions regarding Lake Erie.

"The nature of the fishery on Lake Erie has changed quite a bit," he said. "I hear a lot of complaining about how the fishing is going downhill. That's baloney. The lake is clearing up and the techniques are changing.

"You don't really hear the central basin captains complaining. They've had phenomenal fishing. It's because they've trolled for years. Their fishing has just been getting better.

"Where you hear the complaining is in the western basin, because a lot of the guys there absolutely refuse to get away from weight-forward spinners. There are just fewer and fewer days and conditions when weight-forward spinners work well."

THE FUTURE OF ERIE WALLEYE

Clearer water, and the reduction of pollutants, has allowed oxygen to increase in the bottom of the western basin. Recently mayflies have come back in good numbers, returning an important food source to walleyes. Another result of clearer water and deeper sunlight penetration is the aquatic vegetation that is beginning to show up in harbors and shallow bays.

Lake Erie's walleye population seems to be hanging in at around 50 million fish. Although short of the peak achieved in the mid-1980s, it's an incredible number by any standard.

At this point, fluctuations in the walleye population hinge more on how successfully they spawn than anything else. Only about 10 percent of them spawn in the Maumee and Sandusky rivers. The rest spawn on reefs and hard-bottom shoreline areas. Given favorable weather, Erie's walleye can propagate huge numbers of offspring.

Warm weather in April and May, combined with few storms and cold fronts, produces the best walleye year classes. Heavy storms, on the other hand, generate currents that carry the eggs off the

---

DON'T SPREAD ZEBRA MUSSELS

After boating or fishing on Lake Erie, take steps before leaving to prevent transporting Zebra mussels to other waters. The Sea Grant Advisory Service makes the following suggestions:

—When transporting a boat, drain all bilge water, live wells, and bait buckets before leaving. Leftover bait should not be transported to other waters.

—Thoroughly inspect your boat's hull, outdrive, trim plates, trolling plates, prop guards, transducers, trailers, and other parts exposed to the water. "Hitchhiking" mussels should be scraped off.

—Thoroughly flush hulls, outdrive units, live wells (and pumping systems), bilge, trailer frames, anchors and anchor ropes, bait buckets, raw water engine cooling systems, and other boat parts and accessories that typically get wet using *hot* (140 degree F or hotter) water. Using a pressurized steam cleaner or high pressure power washer would also be effective, require less time, and be environmentally compatible.

—Boats and trailers should be allowed to dry thoroughly in the sun before being transported to uninfested waterways.

—On boats that remain in the water, antifouling paints may be effective in preventing attachment of zebra mussels to boat hulls, outdrive units, propellers, and other underwater boat components and accessories. Consult with your local marine dealer or manufacturer for applicability and local environmental restrictions. Hull waxes do not appear to be effective.

*Mayflies have returned
to the western basin.*

*Trolling often produces more walleyes than
casting methods in Lake Erie's clearer water.*

reefs. Severe cold fronts hold the water temperature down, increasing the incubation period and reducing the odds for a good hatch.

While the number of walleyes fluctuates from year to year, Lake Erie should continue producing excellent fishing. And plenty of these fish will be in the trophy category. In the words of Gary Parsons, who has sampled the best walleye waters in north America, "Lake Erie is absolutely one of the finest fisheries there ever was."

Without question, the title "Walleye Capital of the World" remains firmly in the grasp of Lake Erie.

We must never take Lake Erie's resurgence for granted. While it truly ranks as a remarkable success story, there are still areas of concern, especially with municipal and toxic wastes. If we rest on our laurels and become lax in the battle against pollution and overharvesting by commercial netting, Lake Erie and its walleye could quickly fall from grace.

Chapter 2

Getting on the Water

LAKE ERIE IS nothing to mess with. Anyone who ventures onto this inland sea should do so with a healthy respect for the water and an eye on the weather. It can grow treacherous with harrowing speed.

"I don't ever challenge Lake Erie," says Capt. Andy Emrisko who docks at Cleveland Lakefront State Park, "and I charter out of a 27-foot boat."

Not even the biggest walleye in Lake Erie is worth putting your safety in jeopardy. You would be wise to imitate Emrisko and other sensible charter captains who regularly cancel trips when the forecast calls for heavy seas.

BOATS FOR LAKE ERIE

How much boat do you need for Lake Erie? The minimum would be a 17- to 18-foot deep V hull with, perhaps, a 75 h.p. outboard. This size craft is suitable for calm weather, provided you don't stray too far from shore. It does nicely around the islands in the western basin where you may duck into a port quickly should a sudden storm blow up.

To reach schools of walleyes roaming well offshore in open water, you need something bigger, say, at least a 21- to 23-footer. Center console boats in this size range let four or five anglers spread out from bow to stern when casting and afford ample room on the transom and gunnels for rod holders and other trolling devices. The motor should have enough horses to make the boat get up and gallop. When you see bad weather on the horizon or receive a small craft advisory on your radio, you can't get off the water too fast.

Cruisers in the 25- to 30-foot class handle bigger water and are better suited to offshore

A 17-foot boat is about the minimum for Lake Erie, provided you stay near shore.

The deep, center console rig (foreground) and the big cruiser behind it are capable offshore boats for Lake Erie.

This Stratos 219 DC is one of the new breed of versatile walleye boats.

WALLEYE BOATS

The open boats developed by professional walleye anglers deliver outstanding versatility for many phases of Lake Erie fishing. Most are 18- to 20-foot V hulls constructed from aluminum or fiberglass. The primary outboard, typically 150 h.p. or more, propels the boat at speeds in excess of 50 m.p.h. A small auxiliary outboard, typically 9.9 to 15 h.p., supplies power for trolling and backtrolling. The kicker motor may be rigged so that it steers from the console, but many anglers prefer to sit near the transom and handle a tiller.

Walleye boats are small enough to maneuver easily with a powerful electric motor, especially one that is fixed to the bow. As one fisherman succinctly pointed out, "it's easier to pull a chain than push it."

A bow-mounted electric motor lets you precisely follow irregular bottom contours for casting and slow-trolling presentations, and it will hold the boat in place so you may fish a specific target without anchoring. These are considerable advantages over larger boats,

fishing. Charter captains prefer cruisers with spacious rear decks that let six anglers spread out and cast without interfering with each other. A large rear deck also leaves plenty of room for trolling gear and prevents anglers from tripping over each other to get at a rod when a walleye strikes.

17

The Skeeter 1850 DV handles big water, yet is small enough for a bow electric motor.

which are limited to drifting, anchoring or trolling with a gas motor.

Well designed walleye boats feature ample storage and enough room so that three anglers may fish comfortably. This type of craft is unsurpassed for fishing Lake Erie's reefs, near shore areas and for trolling open water within a reasonable distance from shelter.

Most anglers, however, will find walleye boats too small for trolling several miles from land under anything but tranquil conditions. Walleye professionals often brave wind-driven swells in their boats, but they are a breed caught up in the zeal of competition.

"In an 18-foot glass boat," says accomplished tournament angler Gary Parsons, "I feel comfortable in 6-foot waves. I'm not really intimidated by 8-footers, but I start worrying when storm cells come through. If you get hit with a 40 m.p.h. wind and you're 20 miles off-shore, you might not make it back."

Anybody who doesn't quell in 8-foot waves probably would enjoy riding over Niagara Falls in a barrel.

SAFETY FIRST

Boat maintenance is crucial to safe boating on Lake Erie. Regularly change engine oil, gear case oil, coolants, spark plugs and air, oil and fuel filters. Inspect hoses and replace any that show signs of aging. Check the water level in your batteries frequently and make sure that they are holding a charge.

"Your boat's batteries are especially important," points out Capt. Bob Troxel who docks at Foxhaven Marina on Catawba Island. "If your batteries fail, you lose power *and* the use of your radio. I carry a spare battery, just for insurance."

Check out the slightest hint of a problem, such as a motor that starts hard, stalls at idle, misses or lacks normal power. Neglect your boat and it may leave you dead on the water a long way from safety. Bring extra engine oil, fuses, spark plugs and a tool kit so you can make minor repairs on the water.

Always carry plenty of fuel. Know your boat's range, its fuel consumption by hour. Never gamble. Be sure you have more than enough fuel to reach your fishing water and return. "A good rule of thumb," says Capt. Troxel, "is to divide your total amount of fuel by three: one third out, one third back and one third in reserve."

When boating on Lake Erie, U.S. Coast Guard regulations require that you carry a wearable life jacket for each person on board and a throwable flotation device, such as a seat cushion or life ring.

You also must have a whistle, air horn or power horn, a distress flag, signal flares and a fire extinguisher.

Some state regulations require an anchor large enough to hold the boat and a sufficient length of rope to reach bottom and keep you from drifting. An anchor, of course, doubles as an important fishing tool.

To avoid accidents, learn the basic rules of navigation and use common sense and courtesy when boating on Lake Erie. The western basin, especially, attracts legions of anglers and water-worshippers. For information on proper boating practices, contact

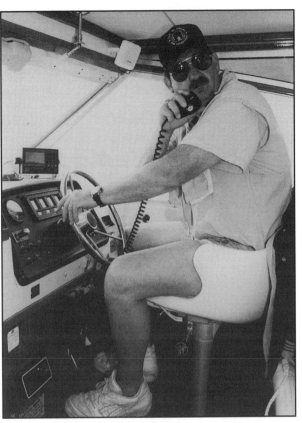

Capt. Bob Troxel prefers a 14-foot antenna for his VHF marine radio.

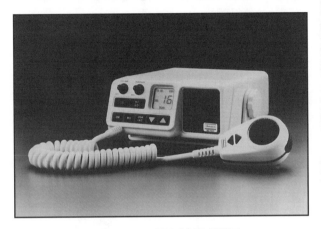

Shakespeare SE-2500 VHF radio has 25 watts of power.

your nearest U.S. Coast Guard office. While you're at it, you may want to register for free safe boating classes.

MARINE RADIO

A VHF marine radio can be a lifesaver if you get caught in dangerous weather, lose your way or find yourself adrift without power. You may call other boaters for help, a towing service or the U.S. Coast Guard, which monitors channel 16.

Another advantage of a marine radio is that you may share fishing information with other anglers. Groups of charter captains routinely contact each other on the water to determine where walleyes are biting and how they are being caught. You may do the same with your friends.

Even when you don't have allies on the water, eavesdropping on other fishermen often provides helpful clues. Listen carefully, however, since many anglers talk in riddles that may be misleading. You may not learn specifically where walleyes are being caught, but you can frequently determine productive methods that will work in your location.

"Invest in a good radio," advises Capt. Eddy Abel, who docks at Spitzer Lakeside Marina in Lorain,

Ohio, "not a little hand-held job that runs on (internal) batteries."

A standard 8-foot VHF marine antenna performs well for boaters who don't travel far from the mainland, perhaps as far out as the Bass islands in the western basin. Those who frequently travel well offshore, such as charter captains, typically rig their boats with taller antennas that deliver greater maximum range and clearer signals.

NOAA WEATHER CHANNEL

Tune into the NOAA weather channel on your VHF marine radio before heading out onto Lake Erie and also while fishing. The station keeps you abreast of current weather and lake conditions, provides forecasts and warns of dangerous weather. It can prevent you from going out when bad weather is advancing and help you get ashore before being caught in a squall.

*A compass, such as this Ritchie
HF-73, is essential on Lake Erie.*

*Flashers are capable depthfinders,
if you can interpret them.*

"I have a 14-foot antenna on my boat," says Capt. Troxel. "It does a nice job. Just remember that some antennas are better than others. Spend the extra money for a quality antenna that has a 6dB to 8dB gain rating."

Bear in mind that a long antenna must be secured at its base and farther up its shaft to so that it stays put in rough water. And don't forget to lower it when passing under bridges as you idle to and from marinas.

CHARTS

Obtain nautical charts for the section of Lake Erie you will be fishing and study them before heading out. This is particularly important when fishing the western basin which has many shallow shoals where you can run aground. Along with fostering safer boating, charts are invaluable for finding and marking productive fishing locations.

Charts are available in large individual sheets or in handy, spiral-bound book formats. They may be purchased at marinas, bait and tackle stores or by contacting the NOAA Distribution Branch, National Ocean Service, 6501 Lafayette Ave., Riverdale, MD 20737. Phone: 301-436-6990.

COMPASS

A marine compass works hand-in-hand with navigation charts, allowing you to avoid shallow, underwater hazards and run true courses that save time and fuel. Anyone who fishes Lake Erie should

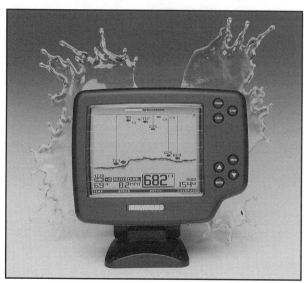

*Liquid crystal graphs, such as this Humminbird
Wide Vision, are especially popular on Lake Erie.*

have a quality marine compass mounted on their boat's console. If you doubt this, try getting back to port without a compass when a dense fog suddenly obliterates landmarks. In this predicament, a compass can guide you to safety.

Carefully read the instructions that come with a compass before installing it. It should be mounted where there is minimal deviation caused by metal objects, switches and gauges. You will have to adjust the compass for deviation after the installation to assure true readings.

DEPTHFINDERS

A depthfinder is indispensable for safe boating and consistent fishing on Lake Erie. This tool tells you when the bottom grows dangerously shallow and reveals the whereabouts of walleyes and the bait fish on which they feed.

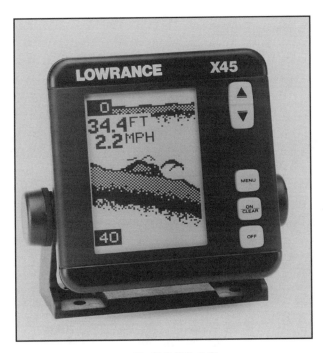

*Lowrance X-45 LCG delivers
good performance at low cost.*

*The GPS module receives
signals from satellites.*

All depthfinders work on the principle of sonar. They send sound waves into the water via a transducer, pick up the signals that bounce back and display them in some way. A digital depthfinder displays numbers and is good only for reading the depth. Flasher depthfinders display the bottom, fish and other objects as lines on a round dial. They provide accurate, detailed information, but some anglers have trouble interpreting the flashes.

Paper, video and liquid crystal displays draw two-dimensional images that many anglers find easier to understand. Graphs also show what has been passed over for several seconds, so you don't miss something if you happen to be looking elsewhere for a moment. This *can* happen with a flasher, which sees only what is directly within the range of the transducer.

While some anglers dote on the superior detail printed by paper graphs, these units are costly to operate if you run them continuously. A few anglers are content with color videos, but videos are bulky and more subject to failure from hard use. Rugged, compact liquid crystal graphs (LCGs), that draw pictures with tiny dots called pixels, have the largest following.

LCGs with the smallest pixels generally produce the highest resolution. They clearly detail the bottom and mark fish of all sizes. Many have other features such as zoom modes, split screens, digital bottom readouts, built-in temperature gauges and more. You can't go wrong with one of the better LCG units when fishing Lake Erie.

Eagle View GPS with plotter.

LORAN & GPS NAVIGATION SYSTEMS

I recall an old cartoon in which one of the characters (Bugs or Daffy, I believe) finds a hot fishing spot in the middle of a vast lake. He catches so many fish that the boat barely floats. Just before leaving, he paints a big "X" on the water to insure that he can return later.

What was humorous not so many years ago has now become reality. Today, Loran and GPS navigation systems, in a sense, paint Xs on the water anywhere you like and accurately return you to them months or even years later.

And there's more. These devices can tell you exactly where you are at any given moment, provide a compass heading that directs you to a specific destination, gauge your running speed and tell you how long it will take to get where you're going. Loran and GPS units with plotters actually draw little maps that show where you've been and where you're headed.

The ramifications of these systems are enormous. You may use them to boat directly to a hot fishing spot or back to a harbor, even at night or through thick fog. Anyone who is serious about catching walleyes on Lake Erie would be foolish not to invest in one of these modern miracles.

Loran—Long Range Navi-

Walleye Pro Mike McClelland hunts for Erie walleyes with a combination GPS/LCG unit made by Lowrance, the LMS 350.

gation—preceded GPS, which is short for Global Position System. Loran is a system based on low-frequency radio waves transmitted from land-based stations. The GPS system, developed by the U.S. Department of Defense, transmits high-frequency radio signals from satellites.

Loran and GPS units must receive their respective radio signals from at least three different sources so they can triangulate the position and display it. Most fishermen prefer to use latitude/longitude instead of time/distance coordinates. Charts are available with latitude/longitude lines that work in conjunction with both Loran and GPS systems.

A given set of coordinates comprise a "waypoint." You may punch in the coordinates for a destination waypoint or instruct the Loran or GPS unit to save the waypoint where the boat is sitting. Most units store a hundred or more waypoints that may be quickly recalled. Once you exceed the unit's memory, you must jot down waypoints down in a notebook.

Probably the first waypoint you should save is the mouth of your home harbor. From there, you can save waypoints for reefs, drop-offs, schools of walleyes or whatever else you find and wish to return to later.

Lake Erie fishermen and charter captains claim that Loran and GPS systems consistently guide them to within 50 yards of their destinations. GPS has the potential to be more accurate, but the military degrades the signals being transmitted to civilian receivers to prevent enemies from taking advantage of it.

Loran receivers cost less than comparable GPS receivers, but they are more susceptible to losing

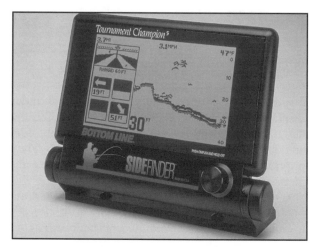

Bottom Line Tournament Champion 5 is a combination LCG and GPS.

signals in bad weather. GPS units, which come down in price every year, rarely fail to pick up signals. Because a GPS unit requires a compact module to receive signals, it is less obtrusive than a Loran, which needs an antenna.

Loran and GPS units that feature plotters offer the greatest advantages for fishing. Say, for example, that you're trolling far offshore and marking your progress on a plotter. You run through a school of walleyes and quickly catch several fish. Using the plotter as a guide, you may circle around, trace your course on the plotter and troll through the same bunch of fish again and again.

Some Loran and GPS plotters feature icons, which are small symbols that you place on the screen

Lowrance Global Map 2000 is an LCG, a GPS and also displays maps.

to mark particular spots. Some units include different icons to represent various locations, such as fish symbols, diamond warning symbols, boat symbols and so on. Veteran walleye professional Mike McClelland finds icons particularly helpful when fishing Lake Erie's reefs with bottom bouncers.

"I may fish an entire reef with a bottom bouncer," says McClelland, "by following a 12-foot contour with my electric motor. As I move along, my plotter draws an outline of the reef. Whenever my bottom bouncer runs across a point, an inside bend or a pod of fish, I punch in an icon to mark that key spot.

"After I've made a complete circle, my plotter shows the exact shape of that 12-foot breakline, plus the icons. I can come back to that reef two years later and call up the information. The plot line will be gone, but I'll see every icon."

Another approach to fishing a reef is to first outline it on the plotter and then fill it in by making systematic trolling passes across the structure. It's an excellent way to make sure that you cover the entire reef.

Some Loran and GPS units combine a LCG with a plotter screen. You may use these units as a depthfinder or a navigation tool, or you may operate both modes at the same time on a split or shared screen.

The most advanced GPS units come with background maps of the entire world. The maps display on the screen and show your exact location on a given body of water. Capt. Al Lesh used one of these devices when I fished with him in the western basin near Luna Pier, Michigan. As we trolled, the screen marked our progress as it related to the shoreline. This would be a great tool for navigating islands in poor visibility.

There is such a vast array of capable GPS and Loran units from which to chose that the selection process can be mind boggling. Don't be discouraged. Once you fish Lake Erie with the help of a Loran or a GPS navigation system, you'll feel lost without it.

HIRING A CHARTER

One of the most relaxing ways to enjoy Lake Erie's walleye fishing is to hire a charter. A typical charter consists of six anglers (that you round up), the captain and possibly a mate. The cost generally runs from about $360 to more than $400 per day.

A recommendation from a friend is one of the most reliable means for finding a good captain. Be sure the captain is licensed by the U.S. Coast Guard and has a guide's license for the appropriate state. Ask for references from his list of clients. The most reputable captains have many repeat customers, so you may have to make reservations eight months or more ahead of time.

Ask plenty of questions when signing on. How long is the trip? What are the hours? What equipment does the captain supply? What do you need to bring?

A deposit is required to hold your date. If foul weather cancels the outing, the captain should reschedule or refund your deposit. If you cancel, you forfeit your deposit.

For casting methods, such as fishing with weight-forward spinners or jigs, you normally bring your own tackle. Narrow your lure selection so that it fits into a small utility type box. There isn't enough room aboard for large tackle boxes. If you'll be trolling, the captain usually supplies the tackle.

In addition to your lunch and beverages, you need to bring adequate clothing and other personal items.

DGPS-READY

If you're considering the purchase of a new GPS unit, be sure that it has "DGPS-ready" circuitry. *Differential* GPS (DGPS) was developed by the U.S. Coast Guard to compensate for the fluctuating accuracy caused by the military's degrading of GPS signals.

DGPS uses land-based stations for additional reference and increases the level of accuracy from 100 meters to 5 to 10 meters or less. Though DGPS is operational only in some areas, the system is expanding. If you purchase a unit that has DGPS-ready circuitry, you'll be able to take advantage of this system when it becomes available.

"Be like a Boy Scout," advises professional walleye angler Rick LaCourse who ran charters on Lake Erie for many years. "Be prepared. Wear loose clothing that you'll be comfortable in. Bring more layers of clothing than you think you'll need. Always bring a jacket and rain gear. Wear soft-soled shoes that won't slip on the deck."

LaCourse also recommends bringing a hat, sunglasses and sunscreen. If you're prone to any type of motion sickness, carry medication to combat the malady. Don't forget appropriate fishing licenses and a camera to record those huge walleyes and beaming faces.

You'll also need a large cooler for transporting your catch at the end of the day and possibly a small cooler for your lunches and beverages aboard the boat. Few captains allow liquor on board, but many allow beer. Be sure to ask your captain his rules concerning alcoholic beverages.

CAPABLE CHARTER CAPTAINS

Capt. Eddy Abel
1019 F St.
Lorain, OH 44052
(216) 288-9995

Capt. Pete Alex,
1134 Payne Ave.
Erie, PA 16503
work: (814) 452-2539
home: (814) 898-0786

Capt. Joe Belanger
4 Young St
Subway, Ont. NOP 2L0
work: (519) 682-0665
hone: (519) 682-1555

Capt. Pat Chrysler
P.O. Box 539
Put-In-Bay, OH 43456
(419) 285-4631

Capt. Dave Demeter &
Dave Demeter Jr.
P.O. Box 274
Lakeside, OH 43440
(419) 798-9195

Captain Andy Emrisko
P.O. Box 27382
Cleveland, OH 44127
(216) 641-2549

Capt. Jim Fofrich
2113 Chase St.
Toledo, OH 43611
(419) 729-2181

Capt. Art Grayling
Glasgow, Ont. RR 3
Rodney, Ont. N0L 2C0
(519) 785-2334

Capt. Ron Johnson
585 Nelmar St.
Painsville, OH 44077
(216) 639-0185

Capt. Bill King
562 Marilla St.
Buffalo, NY 14220
(716) 822-1837

Capt. Al Lesh (fishing instructor)
3811 Los Angeles
Warren, MI 48091
(810) 756-3711

Capt. Jerry Lee
27814 W. Six Mile Road
Livonia, MI 48152
(313) 421-8559

Capt. Dean Thompson
632 Ogden Ave.
Toledo, OH 43609
(419) 382-9444

Capt. Bob Troxel
5517 E. Fox Haven Dr.
Port Clinton, OH 43452
(419) 797-6707

Capt. Phil Whitt
4189 NW Catawba Rd.
Port Clinton, OH 43452
(419) 797-4553

Hiring an experienced guide like Capt. Andy Emrisko is a great way to fish for Lake Erie walleye.

SEA GRANT INFORMATION

The Ohio Sea Grant College Program has many publications and maps that offer a wealth of information to Lake Erie anglers. Among them are:

Twine Line, a bimonthly publication that covers issues, events and research related to Lake Erie. $4.50 per year.

The *Guide to fishing reefs in western Lake Erie*, a detailed chart with reef locations and depths, diagrams of currents, diagrams of the six sport fish that thrive near reefs and tips on when and where to find them. $3.

The *Guide to fishing in central Lake Erie* has charts and other information about conditions that affect fishing success in central Lake Erie. $3.

Contact:
Ohio Sea Grant Publications
The Ohio State University
1314 Kinnear Road
Columbus, OH 43212-1194
(614) 292-8949
FAX: (614) 292-4364

For information related to the eastern basin of Lake Erie contact: New York Sea Grant
101 Rich Hall
State University of New York
Oswego, NY 13126
(315) 341-3042

Chapter 3

Ice Fishing

A RUMOR CIRCULATED a few years ago that a perfetly preserved, frozen mammal was discovered on an ice flow in western Lake Erie. Despite the creature's ape-like, sloping forehead it had unmistakable human features.

Jubilant scientists at first claimed they had found an early predecessor to mankind. Imagine their embarrassment when they learned that their prize was merely a Lake Erie ice fisherman who didn't have enough sense to come in out of the cold.

The above tale may be stretching things a bit, but not by much. In winter, fishermen throughout the Midwest make their way to Lake Erie's western basin like migrating caribou traversing a frozen arctic landscape. Their vehicles cram lakeside parking lots at the tip of Catawba Island and spill out onto the ice. Though Buckeye license plates dominate, on any given day you may see cars and trucks from more than a half dozen states.

These winter anglers forego their warm homes in favor of harsh elements because they know that millions of pre-spawn walleyes have gathered beneath the ice in Lake Erie's island region, including scads of trophy-size fish. And you don't even need a boat to catch them.

WINTER HIGHWAY TO WALLEYES

Many anglers venture forth on foot, their metal grippers crunching a steady rhythm on the ice. They carry augers and plastic 5-gallon buck-ets filled with tackle, or load all manner of sleighs, toboggans and portable shanties with gear and drag them across the hard stuff.

Since walleyes generally lie in deep water a mile or more offshore, foot travel can make for a long, arduous day of fishing, especially in foul weather. Many fishermen opt for the speed and convenience of snowmobiles, all-terrain vehicles and—unbeknownst to their insurance companies—even family sedans.

Be warned that Lake Erie has swallowed up a number of vehicles over the years, as well as anglers who have fallen through the ice. This is no place for the foolhardy.

WINTER CHARTERS

Hiring a reputable charter may be the safest and most reliable means of tapping Erie's winter fishing bonanza. Ice guides frequently relocate to stay on top of walleyes. They also find the safest routes across the ice and provide heated shanties, bait and tackle. You need bring only suitable clothing, food and beverages, and possibly jigging lures. The cost runs about $50 a day per angler.

Dave Demeter's Double D ice fishing service is an offshoot of his popular open-water charter business located at Foxhaven Marina on Catawba Island. A few years ago, I joined him when he hauled a party of six anglers across several miles of ice aboard a pair of snowmobiles towing sleds. The crowds of fishermen gradually

Ohioan Bob Mrugacz jigs for walleyes.

LOCATING WALLEYES

Drilling a hole through the ice in any of the areas recommended in Chapter 14 may put you in touch with walleyes. But normally, it isn't that easy. Pinpointing a school of walleyes usually requires that you move about and check different sites. If one hole isn't producing, you're better off trying a new location than waiting for fish that may never show up.

Depthfinders speed the task of finding fish. Several companies offer portable, battery-powered units with ice fishermen in mind. Two popular flasher models include Zercom Marine's Clearwater Classic Ice System, which features an LCD display, and Vexilar's FL-8, which displays in three colors. Portable, liquid crystal graphs are also available, including several popular models from Eagle.

If the ice is hard and clear, the transducer will shoot through it, saving you the bother of drilling a hole. Place the depthfinder's transducer into a glass cup filled with antifreeze, set the cup on the ice and the depthfinder reveals what lies below. If you forget to bring a cup, gouge a small depression in the ice, fill it with water and then insert the transducer.

Wherever the ice is snow-packed or filled with air bubbles that interfere with a transducer's signals,

Another big walleye slides through the ice at Lake Erie.

thinned the farther we traveled from the mainland. Eventually, we reached Demeter's isolated shanties.

Half of us opted to fish outside in the bright sunlight, while the rest retreated to the cozy warmth of the shanties. Demeter supplied us with short ice fishing rods matched with jigging spoons. We dressed the hooks with minnows.

"It's about 25 feet deep here," said Demeter. "Drop your spoons right to the bottom, reel them up a few inches and jig them once about every 15 seconds."

We proceeded as instructed and soon got into them. I landed a 5-pounder in a matter of minutes. From then on, walleyes bit steadily all day. Several hefty fish piled up around our holes outside. At regular intervals, one or another of the shanty doors opened and a plump walleye sailed out and smacked the ice.

About midday, a commotion in one shanty lasted several minutes. Then came cheers. Moments later, an angler emerged with a walleye weighing over 10 pounds.

you must drill a hole to get a good reading. Pat Chrysler, a prominent ice guide for three decades, has a 4-inch drill for one of his power augers that quickly cuts a small hole for a transducer.

Chrysler operates from his home in Put-In-Bay on South Bass Island. He caters to about 20 anglers a day throughout the season who fly over from the mainland. Finding enough fish for that many people requires a lot of scouting.

"I'll auger two or three hundred holes if I have to," he says, "until I find enough fish for my clients.

"Normally," he says, "you won't find suspended fish in winter, like in summertime. They're going to

Lake Erie ice guide Lenny Banyak isn't bashful about drilling fresh holes.

Zercom's Clearwater Classic is an excellent flasher depthfinder for ice fishing.

be in the bottom third of the water column. They'll be up as far as 12 feet above the bottom if they're really into a heavy feed, like just before an Alberta Clipper rolls through."

Along with locating walleyes initially, a depthfinder helps when actually fishing. You may, for example, be catching fish within 2 feet of the bottom when a walleye swims by 7 feet above your lure. Since lures display prominently on a depthfinder, simply raise your offering up until it shows about a foot above the fish. Walleyes readily move up to take a bait, but rarely swim down to do so.

WHERE NOT TO DRILL HOLES

It's tempting to be drawn to groups of other anglers. After all, would they be there if they weren't catching fish? That may be true, but not necessarily. Walleyes respond to overhead commotion by swimming away. You generally fare better getting away from other anglers and heavily traveled avenues.

"One snowmobile running over your fish," says Chrysler, "can instantly shut down a hot bite. I've seen it happen countless times over the years."

Drilling holes in byways also endangers your fellow fishermen. During periods of thawing, a freshly drilled hole may enlarge to the point where it could trap a tire or, much worse, another angler.

"Never auger a hole," warns Chrysler, "in a road or path. You may only get a quarter inch of ice on it overnight. If you get an inch of snow on top of that, nobody can tell it's there. Fall through one of those and you break your leg."

ICE FISHING TACKLE

Typical ice fishing rods measure about 2 feet in length, which allows them to be used in the confines of a shanty. For outside fishing, some anglers prefer rods measuring 3 feet or more so they don't have to hover so close to the hole. A stiff graphite rod helps detect light bites and embed the hooks.

Light spinning and spincasting reels filled with 6- to 10-pound monofilament match well with ice fishing rods, although 6-pound test is marginal for big walleyes. Clear, low-visibility line persuades more bites in the transparent water.

LURES

Jigging spoons and vibrating blades in 1/4- to 1-ounce sizes comprise the primary ice fishing lures on

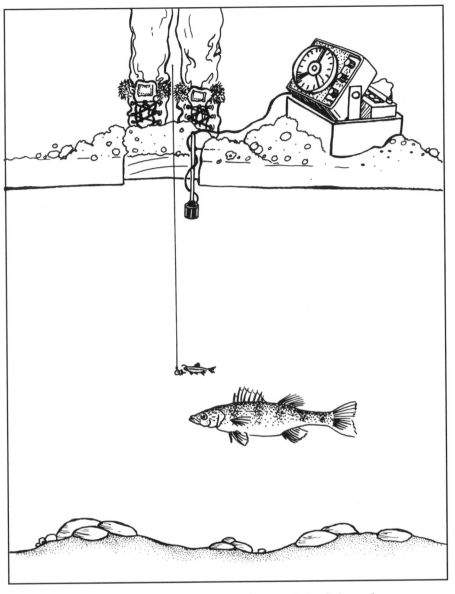

A depthfinder lets you see your lure and the fish, and keep your offering at the right level.

duce. Green and chartreuse patterns are especially popular.

Another exceptional lure is the Pilkki from Rapala, which has single upturned hooks on its nose and tail, a treble underneath and a line loop in the middle of it's back. A clear plastic "fin" on the Pilkki's tail makes it swim out to the side and glide back to center when fished with a lift-drop action.

To avoid line twist with any of these jigging lures, place a small swivel about a foot up the line.

Lures without bait do catch walleyes, but you'll encourage more bites by tipping the hooks with minnows. While lures emit the flash and action that attracts walleyes, it's usually the smell and taste of real meat that cajoles the actual strike.

Minnows, normally 1 1/2- to 2 1/2-inch shiners, hold up well throughout the day because they require little oxygen in the cold water. Bring plenty and lavish them on your lures. Run each point of every hook up through the head of a minnow. A jig-

Lake Erie. Popular spoons include Bay De Noc's Swedish Pimple, the Williams Spoon, Eppinger's Cop-E-Cat, Luhr Jensen's Crippled Herring and Bass 'N Bait's Rattle Snakie. They all feature fluttering actions when worked with lift-drop jigging presentations. The Rattle Snakie is molded around a Pyrex glass rattle that attracts walleyes with sound.

Vibrating blades, such as Heddon's Sonar, Reef Runner's Cicada, Luhr Jensen's Ripple Tail, Bullet Bait's Bullet Blade and Bill Edworthy's Vib "E", also pull many walleyes through the ice. This type of lure gives off a more dramatic vibration when jigged and provides two hooks as opposed to one on spoons.

Plated finishes of gold and nickel are the mainstays for spoons and vibrating blades, but prism tape and painted finishes in a variety of colors also pro-

Clockwise from top left: Swedish Pimple; Cicada; Bullet Blade; Pilkki; Slender Spoon, Rattle Snakie; Cop-E-Cat.

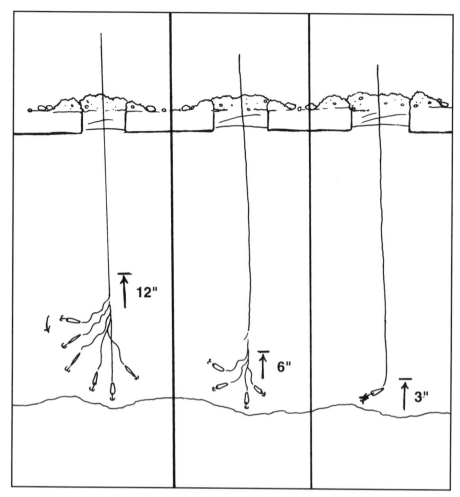

Tip all three points of a treble hook with a minnow.

*Capt. Dave Demeter starts out jigging with a high
lift (left) and gradually decreases the lift and action*

ging spoon rigged with a treble hook should sport three minnows; a vibrating blade with two trebles should bear six.

JIGGING ACTION

Walleyes change moods in winter just as in warmer seasons, so no single jigging action produces every day. Constantly experiment with presentations to determine what the fish want at any given time. If you see suspended fish on a depthfinder, start jigging at their level. Otherwise, consider following the routine that Demeter deploys:

He lets the lure sink all the way down and lifts it just enough so the tails of the bait brush bottom. His first sweep of the rod lifts the lure sharply 12 inches or so, and lets it flutter on a free line to the starting point just above the bottom. After a pause of several seconds, he follows with a lift of 6 inches. After another pause, he lifts the lure only 3 inches.

If no strike occurs after this process has been repeated several times, he lifts the lure with higher sweeps and, again, lets it flutter down on a free line.

If that doesn't trigger a response, he lifts and lowers the lure several times on a tight line, which eliminates the fluttering action.

After that, Demeter makes one crank on the reel, which lifts the lure about 18 inches, and repeats the procedure. He works the lure higher, one crank at a time, until he finds the productive level and action.

"I will go up as high as six or seven reel cranks," says Demeter. "There are a lot of days when we catch fish 10 feet above the bottom."

Ice guide Lenny Banyak, who heads out near Miller's Ferry Landing on Catawba Island, usually works his spoons with shorter pauses than Demeter. He touches the bottom, lifts the spoon 1 or 2 feet and then lets it flutter down. He pauses only a few seconds before repeating the action.

"They inhale it on the drop," he says. "You feel them when you pick up the spoon.

"If I don't get strikes near the bottom, I work the spoon with higher lifts in case they're suspended."

Banyak connects a second treble to a Swedish Pimple, his favorite spoon, by threading it onto the split ring at the tip of the lure. A snap swivel attaches the fishing line to the split ring.

When three minnows adorn each of the two trebles on Banyak's spoons, they must resemble a school of bait fish as they flutter down.

"I catch a lot of walleyes on that top treble hook," he says. "I'm convinced that it catches extra fish for me."

An ice fishing guide for the past 10 years, Banyak drags his shanties out with a snowmobile. Later, after the ice thickens, he cranks up an ancient Chevy flatbed pickup truck. Chains on the tires grip the ice, and empty door hinges afford a quick exit from the cab should the vehicle ever punch through.

For a nominal cost of $5, Banyak also hauls anglers out to productive fishing areas or brings them back to the mainland. Many fishermen eschew his services when trekking out on foot. But after a long hike and several hours of numbing cold, most happily fork over Banyak's fee for the return trip.

If there ever were Lake Erie Eskimos, Banyak would surely be a descendant. He appears to thrive in the bitter environment. No pastel snow suits for this guy. His dark, untrimmed beard forms a wind buffer at the neck of his weathered, tan Cardigans. His omnipresent knit cap hugs his eyebrows.

I once saw him lose a walleye just as he was pulling it up through the ice. He immediately dropped to his belly and jammed an arm deep into the hole in a futile attempt to grab the fish. Minutes later, the outer sleeve of his coveralls froze stiff. Undaunted, Banyak continued fishing as though he were basking in balmy spring weather.

WEATHER & WATER CURRENTS

Even though ice caps the water, the weather very much affects walleyes. The sun, or the lack of it, seems to make little difference, because the fish often bite well on the brightest days. Walleyes react to

When ice gets thick enough in the western basin, ice guide Lenny Banyak hauls clients with an ancient Chevy pickup truck.

A good ice guide provides warm shanties and works hard to keep his clients over walleyes.

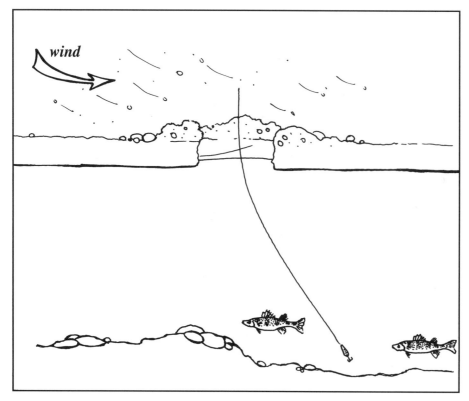

The wind above the ice creates underwater currents.

through the holes, our lines angled sharply to the east. It was extremely difficult to determine when the spoons were on the bottom, let alone work them properly. We stuck with it throughout the afternoon and never caught a fish.

The following weekend, Mrugacz and I again joined Banyak. This time the breeze wafted gently. Though a noticeable current still flowed beneath the ice, it slackened to the point where we could fish effectively with 1/2-ounce spoons. That day we pulled several respectable walleyes through the ice.

SAFETY FIRST

Safety should be your first consideration. Just because you see other anglers out, don't assume that it's all right. Someone else's poor judgment could be your undoing. It requires 6 to 8 inches of ice locked in by the islands to insure reasonable safety in the western basin.

Check with local bait shops and talk with guides to help determine the condition of the ice. Be especially leery of east winds.

"With an easterly wind," says Demeter, "the lake level rises in the western basin, cracking the ice and opening up existing cracks. A crack that may be 3 inches wide on a calm day or on a day with westerly winds may may open up 10 to 12 feet with an easterly wind.

"It's touchy. Extreme caution is necessary anytime."

Strap metal grippers to the soles of your boots to avoid slipping and falls that could result in serious injuries. Wear a life vest when traveling on the ice to insure that you stay afloat should you break through. Bring 50 feet of rope and carry devices that will help you grip the ice and climb out, such as large nails or screwdrivers. Fasten them to opposite ends of a cord and drape the cord over your neck. These items may save you or someone else.

Always travel with at least one companion so help is near in an emergency. And every member of the group should bring a compass. Banyak wears one

weather changes, however, much as they do at other times, feeding ahead of fronts, and growing temperamental immediately after they pass.

The wind drastically affects the fishing. Bear in mind that most of the central and eastern basins remain ice free. Strong winds push the open water, creating currents under the ice.

A stiff current sweeps lures to the side, hampers your ability to manipulate them properly, and to feel the bottom and strikes. Walleyes, sluggish in the cold water, also may prefer not to battle the current in search of food.

Heavier 1-ounce spoons, help combat brisk currents, but don't use them in every situation. Demeter's rule of thumb is, "tie on the lightest spoon the current allows."

"If the current's not running," he says, "light spoons give you a tremendous flutter. The 1/3-ounce Cop-E-Cat has been especially good. I've even dropped to a 1/8-ounce spoon, but you have to go to lighter line to work it right."

The Slender Spoon from Reef Runner is another excellent lure for jigging in light current situations.

I fished with Banyak and my good friend Bob Mrugacz of Johnstown, Ohio, one winter weekend when west winds howled across the lake. Some gusts were so strong they broke shanties lose and pushed them about the ice. When we dropped 1-ounce spoons

Mark Whipple of Fairport Harbor, Ohio, with one of millions of walleyes that gather beneath the ice in Lake Erie's western basin every winter.

on a wrist band. A sudden snow storm can reduce vision to mere feet. Without a compass, you could inadvertently wander away from the mainland and onto fragile ice.

Your body burns enormous amounts of calories in frigid weather sustaining your body heat. Bring plenty of food to fuel your inner furnace and a vacuum bottle filled with soup or a hot drink. Forego alcoholic beverages, which accelerate the lose of body heat.

Sunglasses and sunscreen comprise two of the most overlooked ice fishing essentials. That expansive plane of ice and snow creates a giant sun reflector. On clear, bright days you need protection against the intense rays.

CLOTHING

Modern, cold weather clothing makes ice fishing a reasonably comfortable experience, especially when you dress in layers. Start with long underwear, followed by a warm shirt and pants. Wool garments rate high, because they retain body heat even when wet. Next don a snowsuit that includes a hood. An optional final layer is rain gear, which shields against cutting winds.

Layers of socks also help keep feet warm, provided they don't make your boots fit so snugly that they hinder circulation. Stuff your feet into thick, insulated rubber boots rated for sub-zero temperatures.

Protect your hands with thick mittens, which are warmer than gloves. Bring two pair in case one gets wet. Top the ensemble off with a knit cap. Covering your head is crucial, since this is where the largest percentage of body heat may be lost.

If you bring gear in on foot, avoid breaking a heavy sweat or you'll chill quickly when you stop and fish. Carry some of your clothing with your gear, and put it on after reaching your destination.

OTHER IMPORTANT ITEMS

Plastic, 5-gallon buckets—which you may be able to obtain free from local restaurants or delis. They hold all sorts of ice fishing gear.

One plastic bucket should be reserved for a skimmer to keep holes free of ice, small utility boxes filled with jigging lures, extra line, pliers and a gaff. A gaff is another, often overlooked necessity. Nets don't fit in 12-inch holes. You can't lip walleyes, nor do you want to pull them out by their sharp gill plates.

Many ice fishermen make room in their buckets for warmth-giving gas lanterns that bring feeling back to numb fingers. A 5-gallon bucket also makes a convenient seat when fishing, and nicely carries your catch of big walleyes at day's end.

ICE FISHING REGULATIONS

Ohio fishing regulations prohibit holes in the ice on Lake Erie that have a width greater than 12 inches. Anglers are allowed no more than six tip-ups each. The owner's or user's name and address must be displayed on all tip-ups and ice shelters.

FLY-IN ICE FISHING

Fly-in ice fishing trips to South Bass Island conveniently put you within reach of prime walleye water and some of the safest ice in the western basin. Round trip fare at Griffing's Island Airlines in Port Clinton, Ohio, is currently $32.

Many anglers go over for a day of fishing with a guide, and accommodations are available for extended stays. The guide usually calls the airline and lets them know that you are coming. The flight takes about 20 minutes.

The six passenger, single engine planes have limited room. Most anglers fishing for one day put all their gear in a single 5-gallon bucket. Additional items should be placed in duffel bags for more convenient handling.

Contact Griffing's Island Airlines at (419) 285-3743.

Chapter 4

Jigging Heavy Metal

A HANDFUL OF Lake Erie anglers catch walleyes with jigging spoons and vibrating blades throughout the season. Most anglers, however, opt for these heavy metal lures only during the cold-water period that begins in fall, runs through winter (whether fishing through the ice or in open water) and ends in spring when the water temperature climbs near 50 degrees.

Since ice fishing is covered elsewhere in this book, this chapter deals with *open-water* jigging with heavy metal lures. In cold-water conditions, it's like ice fishing without the ice. There are no holes to drill, but you still jig vertically for sluggish walleyes in deep water. Fishing from a boat provides the advantage of greater mobility.

Even though you may be skilled with the traditional jig and minnow, there will be days when jigging spoons and vibrating blades—also called blade baits—trigger more strikes. These lures deliver a fluttering action and an alluring shimmer that resembles a dying minnow. To a Lake Erie walleye, they are a flashing neon sign that reads "FREE MEAL."

Basic jigging methods with spoons and vibrating blades are fairly easy to master. If you're serious about making the most of your cold-water outings, give these heavy metal lures a high priority.

HEAVY METAL

Most jigging spoons for walleyes feature narrow tips and wider tails. Some are molded, while others are stamped. They tend to have a

slow fall and a lively wobble. For the most part, they include the same 1/4- to 1-ounce lures employed for ice fishing: Bay De Noc's Swedish Pimple, the Williams Spoon, Eppinger's Cop-E-

Heavy metal lures score in open water.

Clockwise from top left: Cicada tipped with plastic; Swedish Pimple; Crippled Herring; Rattle Snakie; Ripple Tail; Vib "E".

Cat, Luhr Jensen's Crippled Herring, Bass 'N Bait's Rattle Snakie, and the Slender Spoon from Reef Runner.

A flat or cupped blade in the shape of a minnow comprises the heart of the vibrating blade. The head and belly of the lure—lead in most cases—is molded to the blade. One treble hook attaches to the belly, another to the tail. A hole in the lure's back holds a snap for your line. Some vibrating blades have two or three holes that let you adjust the pulsating action. You really feel this lure vibrate when you lift it with the rod.

Popular blade baits on Lake Erie weigh from 1/2 to 3/4 ounce and include Heddon's Sonar, Luhr

Jensen's Ripple Tail, Bullet Bait's Bullet Blade (constructed from light zinc alloy), Bill Edworthy's Vib "E" and Reef Runner's Cicada. To avoid line twist, attach a 2-way swivel about a foot above blade baits, especially those with cupped blades, such as the Cicada and Ripple Tail.

Bright metal finishes in spoons and blade baits score well, typically nickel, gold and copper in that order. Embellishing these lures with prism tape effectively adds color. Painted finishes in chartreuse and perch patterns also deserve a place in your tackle box.

For cold-water jigging, always tip spoons and blade baits with minnows. Skewer 1 1/2- to 2-inch minnows by running the hooks up through their jaws and out the tops of their heads. A single minnow may suffice in some instances. At other times, you'll entice more bites by tipping each point of a treble hook with a minnow. Most vibrating blades hold up to six minnows.

ADVANTAGES OF ANCHORING

Dancing spoons and blade baits on or just above the bottom is the most widely used tactic for cold-water walleyes. Keep the line as straight up and down as possible to improve lure control, afford a livelier lure action and enhance strike detection. Fishing from an anchored boat maintains vertical lines and lets you work one spot long enough to coax strikes from lethargic fish.

Before dropping anchor, scout for walleyes with a depthfinder. In late fall and early spring, concentrate

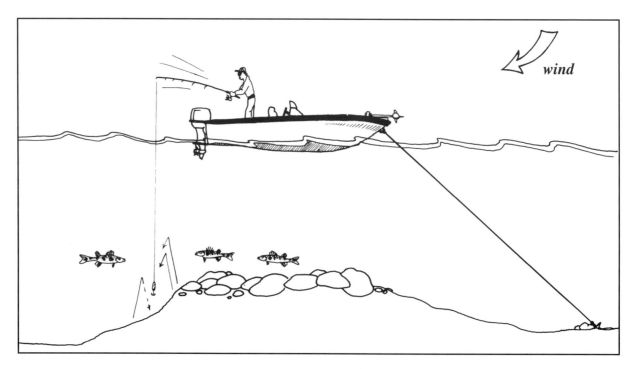

Jigging from an anchored boat early in the season is similar to ice fishing.

on water 25 to 35 feet deep near spawning areas, particularly in the western basin. Vast numbers of walleyes congregate in such places at these times. Once the spawn commences, also check out the edges of spawning reefs 15 to 25 feet deep. In depths much shallower than 15 feet, vertical jigging is less effective.

Study your depthfinder closely, because walleyes often hold so tight to the bottom that they are hard to distinguish. When you begin marking fish that have potential, drop anchor. You won't know for certain you are marking walleyes until you begin catching them.

Let your lure fall straight down from the rod tip to the bottom. Crank it up a few inches. Then lift it 1 or 2 feet and let it fall back on a semi-tight line. As the lure flutters down, the minnows on the hooks slow the fall and undulate like a small school of bait fish. Let the lure rest above the bottom for several seconds between each lift. Most strikes occur as the lure drops or during a pause.

Walleyes may suspend 6 feet or more above the bottom, so crank the lures up a few feet at a time and jig at higher levels until you get into them. Keep an eye on the depthfinder, since it may mark suspended walleyes and reveal the proper depth.

RIG A STILL ROD

Simple arithmetic shows that the more baits or lures you have in the water, the better your odds for tempting walleyes. Most Lake Erie anglers fish with

Ron Perrine lands a Lake Erie walleye taken on a Rattle Snakie spoon.

two rods at a time when trolling. Relatively few, however, use more than one rod when jigging. Accomplished anglers effectively jig with one rod in each hand, which is not nearly as difficult as it sounds. Lifting and dropping both rod tips in unison helps avoid confusion. If you're ever in doubt as to which lure has been bit, set the hook with both rods.

Another effective ploy for doubling your odds is using a still rod, which some anglers call a *dead stick.* This involves resting one rod in a holder while jigging another rod by hand. To some, the still rod appears to be a whim, but experienced anglers know that it can be deadly. As the boat lifts and drops on the waves, the rod in the holder imparts a natural jigging action to the lure.

I received my first lesson on fishing with still rods several years ago during an early spring outing on the western basin shortly after ice-out. The air and water temperature were both in the mid-30s and the fish were deep and sluggish. Despite bright sunshine and a snowmobile suite, running over the water in an open boat was decidedly "brisk."

It was my good fortune to be with Phil Whitt, a charter captain who manages Beach Cliff Lodge on Catawba Island, and Dave Demeter Jr., who runs charters out of nearby Foxhaven Marina. We dropped anchor near one of Lake Erie's famous Bass Islands

Ron Perrine, maker of the Rattle Snakie spoon, jigs for walleye on Lake Erie.

Charter captain Dave Demeter Jr. with a Lake Erie walleye taken on a "dead Stick." Note the rod in the holder behind him.

and began vertically fishing jigging spoons tipped with minnows. We worked the spoons near bottom 35 feet deep, and gave them gentle lifts between long pauses of 10 seconds or more. Anything faster would not entice the cold, lethargic fish.

Whitt and I used one rod apiece, but Demeter placed a second rod in a holder so that it rested parallel to the water's surface. I figured he was using the holder so he could stuff his free hand into the warmer wrapped around his waist. I didn't realize he was also trying to determine if the walleye wanted an idle spoon that was better presented with a still rod.

While we all managed to catch some nice walleyes that day, weighing up to about 7 pounds, Demeter's still rod accounted for the most fish. I was stunned. I had presumed that the light bites would be hard to detect without actually holding the rod, and that it would be difficult to respond in time to set the hook with the rod in a holder. I was wrong on both counts.

With the still rod in a horizontal posture, we could all see the tip bend down unmistakably when a walleye nabbed the spoon, especially when the boat rode up on a swell. When a strike occurred, Demeter immediately snatched the rod from the holder and drove the hooks home. The effectiveness of the still rod was undeniable.

DRIFTING

If you just can't seem to get in touch with walleyes by anchoring, try jigging while drifting.

Though it's impossible to maintain vertical lines while moving, a slow drift keeps lures close enough to the boat for an effective presentation. You may repress the drift with a sea anchor when a breeze pushes you along too fast. Heavy lures, up to 1-ounce, also stay closer to a drifting boat than lighter lures.

Drifting lets you cover more area and find a concentration of walleyes over which you may then anchor. When walleyes are scattered, drifting allows you to pick off individual fish. This method works well when fishing large areas that have featureless bottoms. When following the contours of reefs and other structures, an electric motor or small outboard lets you make adjustments and sustain controlled drifts. Scott Stecher, president of Reef Runner Lures, prefers this approach when drifting western basin reefs.

"The drop-offs of reefs," says Stecher, "are especially good for blade baits in the spring. I like the bigger reefs, like Flat Rock and Cone, where you can cover a 15- to 22-foot edge for a mile and catch walleyes all the way through the drift. Walleyes spread out all over those reefs."

As he drifts with the breeze, Stecher casts a Cicada a short distance ahead of the boat. Because his boat moves into the cast, the lure sinks quickly to the bottom without any drag. A lure cast upwind behind a boat is pulled by the drift. It sinks slowly and swims higher and farther with each rod lift.

Thanks to the short cast, Stecher may jump the Cicada off the bottom with short, 12-inch rod lifts and

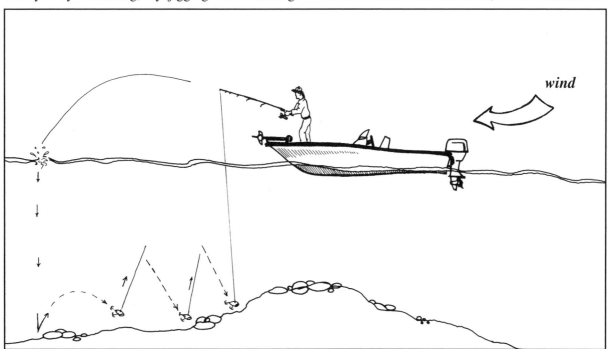

Scott Stecher, president of Reef Runner Lures, prefers to drift with the wind, cast ahead of the boat and work a Cicada back with short hops.

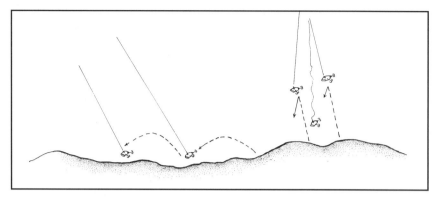

Long casts swim jigs and blade baits over the bottom (left).
Short casts result in sharper, more productive lifts (right).

transmit a distinct up and down action. When a spoon or blade bait has been cast a long distance, it tends to swim ahead when you lift the rod tip. It doesn't begin jumping up until it gets close to the boat as the line becomes more vertical.

"When the lure gets back to the boat," says Stecher, "you vertically jig it a couple of times, crank it up and pitch it downwind again."

In light winds, Stecher goes with a 1/4- to 3/8-ounce Cicada. If the wind picks up, he increases to a 1/2-ounce size. He generally fishes these lures on 6-pound test monofilament, which helps them sink faster and reduces line bagging. The Cicada features two double hooks in place of trebles, which cuts down

on snags. Even so, most anglers will have fewer problems with 8- or 10-pound test line, especially when fishing reefs that tend to gobble up bottom-bouncing lures.

SUMMER JIGGING

Casting ahead of a drifting boat also produces walleyes for Stecher when he visits the central basin during the summer. Walleyes are more active and agile in the warmer water and often respond to more vigorous jigging. Sometimes ripping a heavy metal lure 3 to 4 feet at a pop is what it takes to capture a walleye's attention.

When walleyes respond to aggressive jigging actions, you may forgo live bait. The fish are feeding by sight and striking by reflex. Scent can't hurt, but it really doesn't help.

"To add color and even more action to a Cicada," says Stecher, "I break the tail off a chartreuse or brown (Berkley) Power Bait and thread it on the back hook. You should see that thing come alive in the water."

When summertime walleye are in a more pensive mood and demand a subtle jigging presentation,

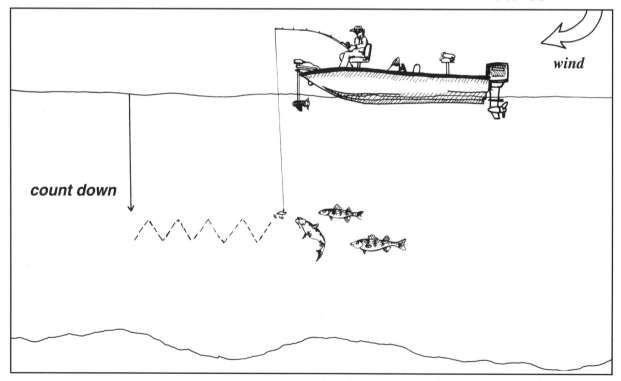

Blade baits and jigging spoons will take suspended walleyes. Cast them out, count
them down to the desired depth and work them back with a lift-drop action.

Stecher breaks off a chunk of a crawler and tips the front set of hooks. The scent of real meat can make a big difference.

"I've caught a lot of fish on blade baits in the central basin," says Stecher. "I've taken suspended fish 45 feet deep in 60 to 80 feet of water by casting ahead of the drift and counting the lure down like you would a weight-forward spinner."

TACKLE

Both spinning and baitcasting outfits do an excellent job of serving up jigging spoons and blade baits. These lures cast extremely well. You don't really cast them at all when vertical jigging—simply let them drop straight down over the side of the boat on a free line.

The rod should have plenty of backbone, say a medium to medium-heavy action. Get a graphite rod for more sensitivity. You can't go wrong with a 6- to 6 1/2-footer.

Walleye champion Mark Brumbaugh nets a Lake Erie walleye for Scott Stecher. The fish went for a Cicada.

Ohioan Don Sibley hefts a Lake Erie Walleye taken by counting down a blade bait.

Chapter 5

Jig Fishing

WHEN MILLIONS OF walleyes swarm western basin reefs and shorelines to spawn in early April, they set the stage for a month of more of prime jig fishing. And don't overlook the miles of productive shorelines in the central basin near Vermilion and Lorain.

So many walleyes frequent these spawning structures that drifting over them haphazardly while casting or dragging jigs almost guarantees at least a few fish. Consistently catching limits, however, requires the ability to pinpoint key locations, maneuver a boat with precision and work jigs with a refined presentation. Gary Roach of Merrifield, Minnesota, the venerable walleye professional who initiated reef fishing on Lake Erie, qualifies as a master on all counts.

"Walleyes prefer to spawn on the highest peaks of the reefs," explains Roach. "Some of Erie's reefs are huge, and they don't drop off real fast.

"There may be a large area of bottom 15 feet deep, then it comes up to 7 feet or 5 feet. The key humps are the ones that have the most gravel and rock."

Roach acknowledges that walleyes back out to the edges of drop-offs on the reefs, especially in clear-

water conditions or when assaulted by heavy fishing pressure. While zebra mussels have increased the water clarity, this portion of the western basin is often stained in the spring due to the muddy runoff carried in by the Maumee River. Bottom sediments stirred up in the shallows by the wind also add to the murk.

"Much of the time," says Roach, "you're not seeing more than 8 inches into the water. You don't want it too clear. As the water gets clearer, the walleyes move closer to the edges."

Males weighing up to about 6 pounds comprise most of the walleyes taken from the reefs. Bigger females generally move up at night, drop their eggs, and then quickly slide back out to deeper water before they are caught.

Frank A. Scalish

NIGHTTIME JIGGING UNNECESSARY

Given the walleye's nature to move up on spawning sites at night, particularly the females, it seems that better catches could be made fishing these structures on Lake Erie after dark. Roach agrees.

"That's the way of the walleye," he says. "The big fish move up at night. In Minnesota, they'll fish all night long to catch big walleyes.

"But on Lake Erie, there's no need to lose any sleep. How many fish do you want to catch? It gets ridiculous after awhile. If you can't catch walleyes in Lake Erie in the daytime, with as many of them that gang up shallow in the spring, you better go golfing."

CONTROLLED DRIFTING

Under calm daylight conditions, Roach drifts over reefs with his 20-foot Lund walleye boat. He employs a transom-mounted electric motor to quietly adjust the boat's position. His relatively small, maneuverable craft has a distinct advantage over larger boats when he fishes reefs. Adjusting the drift with, say, a 25-foot cruiser requires starting the gas motor, which can disturb walleyes in the shallows.

A 1/8-ounce pink and white jig produces best for Roach in most reef fishing situations on Lake Erie. He often dresses the jig with a Berkley Power Grub and always tips the hook with a 2 1/2- to 3-inch minnow. "They definitely have a preference for minnows in cold water," adds Roach.

YO-YO JIGGING

Wielding a spinning rod matched with 6-pound test line, Roach works the lure with a technique he

Walleye sage Gary Roach initiated spring jig fishing on western basin reefs.

calls *yo-yo jigging*. Essentially, it consists of lifting and dropping the jig along the bottom while keeping it near the boat.

"The fish are tight to the bottom," says Roach. "You've got to tap the bottom, swim the jig within 2

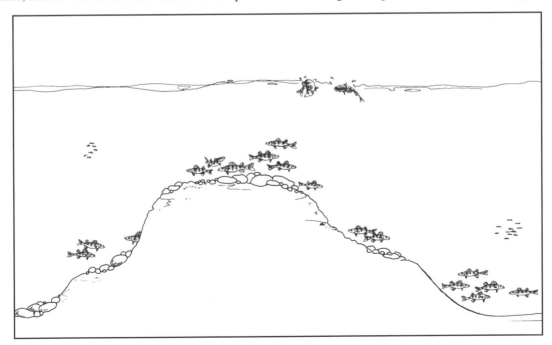

Every spring, the spawning ritual draws millions of walleyes to reefs and areas near shore in Lake Erie's western basin.

When fishing jigs, Gary Roach sits near the transom and maneuvers the boat with a small kicker outboard or an electric motor.

feet of the bottom and tap the bottom again. Work the jig too high, and you won't catch a fish. Drag it on the bottom without lifting it, and all you'll catch is snags."

The Zebra mussels that now encrust the reefs fill many crevices which cuts down on snagging. But zebras have sharp edges that can slash your line when battling a walleye. The more line you let out, the more likely this is to occur.

SLOW AS A RULE

"Speed control is crucial," says Roach. "A slow drift is best. That's where most fishermen run into problems. They let the wind push them so fast that their jigs zip over the bottom. The walleyes can't react in time."

When the wind increases to the point that Roach has trouble maintaining a slow drift, he puts out a sea anchor from the bow with 6 feet of rope. Also called a drift sock or wind sock, this device is essentially a huge canvas or nylon bucket that has a hole in the bottom. It creates substantial breaking power and slows a boat's drifting speed. Roach was one of the first to use drift socks on Lake Erie. They have since grown quite popular here, especially with charter captains.

When attached to the bow, a drift sock helps hold the boat broadside to the wind. It should always be fastened to the windward side. Even with the drift sock out, Roach still manipulates the boat with a transom-mounted electric motor. In extremely windy conditions, he resorts to the small gas kicker next to his primary outboard.

The drift sock also improves boat control under blustery conditions when Roach backtrolls using the kicker motor. Backtrolling affords the same jig presentation as when drifting, with the advantage that the

angler may move in any direction. The wind and waves reduce the negative effects that outboard noise may have on walleyes. Splash guards on the boat's transom prevent waves from washing in.

"The sock," says Roach, "keeps the bow of the boat from being blown downwind like a flag. It lets me backtroll in any direction and maintain control."

Another proponent of drift socks is Keith Kavajecz from Chilton, Wisconsin, one of the most renowned professional walleye anglers in the country. He prefers to put a drift sock out near the transom and position his Tracker walleye boat broadside to the wind with a bow-mounted electric motor.

"I like smaller 48-inch sea anchors," says Kavajecz. "When drifting over shallow reefs, larger sizes create such turbulence that they can actually spook walleyes. If the wind gets up over 20 m.p.h., I'll put out another sea anchor about half way up the gunnel. That will handle just about anything you want to stay out in. I have run as many as three sea anchors in severe winds."

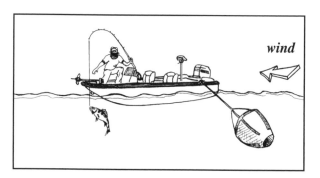

A drift sock slows a boat's drift.

PRECISION CASTING

Many anglers fare better when wind, waves and muddy water batter the reefs, because walleyes are more tolerant of boats during turbulent weather. Calm, clear water drives walleyes deeper and makes them boat shy. Under these more amicable weather conditions, Kavajecz scores well by casting jigs as he eases his boat into the breeze with a bow-mounted electric motor. Before ever making the first cast to a reef, however, he idles over it while intently studying his liquid crystal graph.

"There isn't any key depth," says Kavajecz. "Crib, Niagara, Toussaint, all the reefs are different. Some come up to 4 and 5 feet; others only come up to 10 feet.

"One key place is the shallowest part of the reef, but most of the time I do better fishing the edges. I look for knobs, fingers and lips that have a little sharper drop."

Upon finding a likely ledge, Kavajecz saves the location as a waypoint on his GPS. When his sonar reconnaissance is finished, he thoroughly fishes only the specific locations he has marked, not the entire expanse of a reef.

Maneuvering his bow into the wind or quartering across it, Kavajecz inches ahead while keeping his boat positioned over the targeted structure break. Lobbing short 20- to 30-foot casts ahead of the boat, he covers the top, side and bottom of the break. Once the walleyes reveal their preference, say at the top edge, Kavajecz concentrates on that particular level.

In many instances, the windy side of a reef attracts a concentration of walleyes. In this case, Kavajecz holds the boat directly above the wind-blown edge, casts into the wind and works the jig up the drop. When the wind blows too hard to hold the boat, Kavajecz moves off the deep side of the drop and anchors from the bow. From this position, he casts up onto the reef and works his jig down the drop.

ANCHORING

Anchors take the work out of maintaining your position. They also comprise the only means of staying put with boats that are too large to be maneuvered with an electric motor or an auxiliary outboard. Fishing from an anchored boat lets you stay with a school of walleyes and employ slower jig presentations than are possible from a moving boat.

On any given day, for who knows what reason, walleyes may show a strong preference for jigs inched over the bottom or fished vertically (straight down) with little movement. Vertical presentations are essential for sluggish, pre-spawn walleyes in cold water. You simply must give the walleyes plenty of time to inspect your lure and strike.

Anchor small boats from bow to prevent waves from washing over their transoms. In heavy seas, this also should be done with larger boats. Many charter captains, however, anchor their cruisers from the stern in moderate seas. This reduces the boat's inclination to swing back and forth.

A CASE FOR LIGHT JIGS

"On those shallow reefs," says Kavajecz, "you want to go as light as you can and still feel the bottom. On a real calm day, I go down to a 1/16-ounce pink and white jig with a 2-inch curly-tailed grub. When it's windy, I move up to 1/8-ounce jig. It has to get super windy before I tie on a 1/4-ounce jig.

Walleye pro Keith Kavajecz prefers to stand when casting jigs to Erie's reefs.

"For reef fishing, I've had my best luck tipping the hook with a minnow, or a half or even a third of a crawler. Use too big a crawler, and they pluck it right

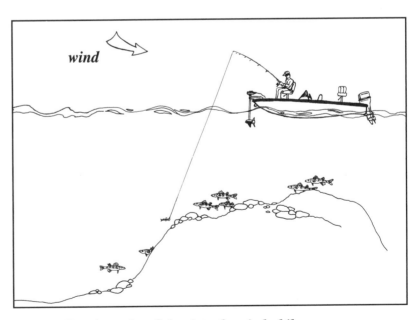

Kavajecz often fishes into the wind while maneuvering the boat with a bow-mounted electric motor.

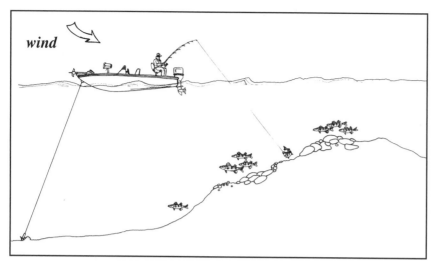

Casting jigs downwind from an anchored boat is deadly, especially after locating a school of walleyes on a reef.

transom, typically a 9.9 to 15 h.p. Mercury. He puts the motor in forward gear, locks it straight ahead and then moves to the bow and steers the boat with the electric motor. Use extreme caution if you employ this tactic. Never try it while fishing alone and always wear a life vest.

"That little kicker motor," says Kavajecz, "makes a huge difference. I run it at idle speed or a little faster, just enough to compensate for the wind. All the electric motor does is position the boat. It doesn't have to push into the wind. You have more control and you don't drain your batteries."

off your jig. With a 1/16-ounce jig, a walleye easily sucks the hook into it's mouth. With heavier jigs, they often get just the tail of your bait."

Northland's FireBall jig gets the nod from Kavajecz when he's casting to reefs. He claims that the FireBall's short, wide-gapped hook holds the bait close to the jig's head and insures solid hookups with horizontal presentations.

Kavajecz ties limp, 6-pound line to the jig, usually Berkley Select, and casts it with a short 5 1/2-foot Team Daiwa graphite spinning rod. Since short casts are the rule with this tactic, a longer rod isn't necessary. More important, Kavajecz firmly believes that short rods deliver maximum sensitivity.

"A walleye," he says, "won't crunch down on your jig and swim around with it. If he senses that something is wrong, he blows it right back out. You have a very short amount of time to detect the bite and set the hook."

After making a cast, Kavajecz lets the jig settle to the bottom on a tight line. He then lifts the rod tip to the 11 o'clock position and holds it dead still. This pulls the jig up and allows it to pendulum back to the bottom. Maintain a tight line as the jig falls to insure the immediate detection of strikes. While most strikes come during the fall, walleyes sometimes inhale the jig from the bottom. In this instance, you normally feel a mushy sensation as you lift the jig. When in doubt, don't hesitate—set the hook!

Be sure to continue the pendulum retrieve all the way back to the boat. Many strikes, says Kavajecz, occur just before you reel the jig strait up from the bottom. He believes these come from fish that follow the jig in and sense that their quarry is getting away.

Should the wind grow too strong for the electric motor, Kavajecz starts the kicker outboard on the

Keith Kavajecz carries a wide assortment of jigs and generally opts for lighter sizes.

The short-casting methods that work so well for Kavajecz on Lake Erie's reefs are basically the same approaches he developed when fishing structure on other bodies of water. On Lake Erie, however, there is one notable difference.

"There are just so many more fish," emphasizes Kavajecz. "If you get out on Erie's reefs in favorable

Keith Kavajecz is pleased that this Lake Erie walleye found a jig to its liking.

conditions during April and early May, catching 50 to 100 walleyes a day is fairly easy.

"Once you find a key little spot, you can just hang right there and catch 10 to 15 fish before you've got to move on. Then you can come back later and catch more."

A CASE FOR HEAVY JIGS

Although light jig presentations work well in clear water, Kavajecz admits that he learned something from Lake Erie charter captains when muddy water persists. Under these conditions, charter captains rely on a comparatively heavy 1/4-ounce jig dressed with a 3-inch chartreuse, curly-tailed grub, as opposed to the 2-inch size Kavajecz normally uses.

The larger, heavier jig generates more vibration, especially when it bumps bottom. Walleyes have an easier time locating the noisier package when their vision is impaired, and they more easily see bright colors, such as chartreuse.

"In murky water," says Kavajecz, "the walleyes in Erie revert to their sense of feel. You need an aggressive action that sends out more vibrations. That's when I rip the jig up and let it smack the bottom."

Clockwise from top: FireBall jig with stinger; Fuzz-E-Grub; Lipstick jig, big grub & heavy jig; Jumbo Fuzz-E-Grub; Jumbo Hummer.

Stained water normally accompanies strong winds, which dictates a low rod tip. If you hold the rod high, the wind bags your line and hampers lure control. Dropping the rod close to the water reduces the effects of the wind on the line. Work the jig over the bottom by sweeping the rod tip parallel to the water, or, hold the rod low, crank a few times and stop. Both ploys lift the jig off the bottom and let it swing back down in the correct fashion.

A low rod tip also should be applied whenever you drag or troll a jig. Kavajecz resorts to these approaches when fishing water deeper than 10 feet. In calm conditions, he trolls quietly ahead under the power of a bow-mounted electric. When it's windy, he may drift or troll with the kicker outboard.

"I think of drifting and jig trolling as a moving cast," says Kavajecz. "I sweep the rod sideways and let the jig pendulum to the bottom. As the boat moves along, I let my rod drift back and then I sweep the jig forward again."

Heavier jigs prevail when Kavajecz drifts and trolls, typically 1/4- and 3/8-ounce sizes. The additional weight stays on bottom and maintains a more vertical presentation. The line should swing back no more than about 45 degrees.

As when casting, Kavajecz dresses the jig with a curly-tailed grub and tips it with a minnow or a piece of a crawler. Due to the more vertical presentation, he feels he gets better hook ups with a jig that features a longer shank, such as Northland's Lipstick jig.

DRIFTING ATTITUDE

Dragging jigs in the spring also is a mainstay for Capt. Dave Demeter, who operates Double D charters out of Foxhaven Marina on Catawba Island, Ohio. Setting up a successful drift, especially with larger fishing boats like Demeter's 30-foot cruiser, requires an intimate knowledge of how the boat responds to the wind. Every boat displays unique characteristics in this respect.

Boats featuring high sides catch more wind and drift faster than those designed with low sides. Some boats drift broadside and maintain a true line, while most tack fore or aft. Anglers who don't know how their boats perform while drifting continually miss targeted areas or repeatedly have to start their engines and make adjustments.

Demeter's seamanship and his intimate knowledge of Lake Erie's reefs, shallow beaches and rocky shoreline structures helps him hit his marks consistently when dragging jigs tipped with minnows. He carries a large drift sock to slow his drift if need be. When he locates a concentration of fish, he drops anchor and works on them.

BOMBARDING BEACHES

Capt. Dean Thompson, who runs out of Minky's West Marina in Toledo, Ohio, dotes on the beaches from Crane Creek west to Maumee Bay, and on the humps in Maumee Bay created by dredgings left along the edge of the shipping channel. Here, zebra mussels cover the sand and muck bottom, substantially increasing the spawning habitat for walleyes.

Because the water tends to stay quite murky in this area throughout the spring, walleyes frequent depths ranging from as shallow as 3 feet to about 17 feet of water. On most days, the same question crackles from marine radios: "How deep are you pulling your fish?"

Once a productive depth is determined—through radio communication or trial and error—Thompson drifts beaches and humps along that contour while bombarding walleyes with 1/2- to 1-ounce jigs dressed

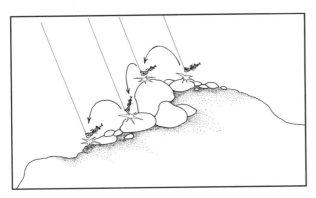

Capt. Dean Thompson and Ted Takasaki bounce heavy jigs on the bottom in the western basin.

with 4-inch, curly-tailed grubs. He works the heavy jigs with a fast, bottom-smacking presentation.

"That's our style at this end of the lake," says Dean. "We call it the three-crank or four-crank.

"You cast downwind and keep your line tight. When the line goes slack, you know your jig's on the bottom. You crank three or four times and stop. As soon as the jig hits bottom, crank three or four times again and stop. Keep that routine going as fast as you can work the reel.

"That jig just goes *bang-bang-bang-bang* over the bottom. When there's any break in the rhythm, set the hook and you'll be fast to a walleye."

Casting downwind prevents the boat's drift from slowing the jig's fall. Match the heavy jigs with spinning or baitcasting tackle and 8-pound test line.

DEEP JIGGING

Male walleyes provide good fishing on the reefs well into May for Demeter, though he generally must fish deeper as the water clears. The influence of zebra mussels cannot be avoided.

"Walleyes used to spawn," says Demeter, "from the tops of the reefs down to about 8 to 10 feet. But now I find that I'm catching more fish by staying off the edges of the reefs in 12 to 25 feet of water. Either we just discovered that they're spawning deeper, or they're spawning deeper because of the clearer water."

When the big post-spawn females come off the reefs, Demeter believes they first hug bottom in 25 to 35 feet of water. Eventually they perk up and feed on suspended bait fish, availing themselves to trolling tactics and weight-forward spinners. Until then, they remain susceptible to drift fishing with jig and min-

now combinations.

"We do a lot of jig fishing in deep water," says Demeter. "Just drifting and long-lining a 1/2-ounce jig with a big minnow hooked through the nose. Just bounce it slowly off the bottom."

JUMBO JIGGING

Probing the depths with heavy jigs is nothing new to Ted Takasaki of Algonquin, Illinois. When this capable walleye professional visits the western basin in the spring, he often scores well on post-spawn walleyes with a technique he calls "jumbo jigging."

His primary jigs include 5/8- and 1-ounce Jumbo Fuzz-E-Grubs and Jumbo Hummers that feature spinner blades on their collars, both made by Lindy-Little Joe. These lures feature capable 2/0 hooks, which Takasaki tips with a 2 1/2- to 3-inch minnow or a whole, fat night crawler impaled once through the nose. He uses a whole crawler because he's after big walleyes.

Bright colors, such as orange, chartreuse and hot chartreuse (a glow color) produce best on Lake Erie when Takasaki drops his jumbo jigs into the dark depths on 12-pound test Stren Magnathin line. The line peels off a baitcasting rod seated on a stiff flippin' rod normally used by bass anglers for heavy cover. Again, it's obvious that Takasaki has big fish in mind.

"I've caught fish jumbo jigging on Lake Erie," says Takasaki, "anywhere from 18 feet all the way down to the 50 foot range. You don't always have to mark fish down on the bottom for it to work, but you do have to have structure. That includes the edges of reefs and the deep portions of reefs. I've done especially well on reefs north of Kelleys Island, for example."

Some of these deep-water structures are subtle and easy to overlook. In one major walleye tournament, Takasaki once caught the biggest first day limit by jumbo jigging a 200-yard hump that rose from 50 feet of water to 45 feet and back down to 50 feet.

"The important thing," says Takasaki, "is that you go slow enough to maintain bottom contact. I usually drift or pull the boat along with an electric motor. If I need to, I use a wind sock to help me slow down."

If you can't feel bottom when jumbo jigging, you're either moving too fast or using a jig that is too light. Go with a 5/8-ounce jig in 10 to 25 feet of water. A 1-ounce size covers a range from about 25 feet to 50 feet. Methodically lift and drop the jig 6 to 8 inches over the bottom while keeping the line as vertical as possible.

"When the jig hits bottom," says Takasaki, "you should feel a real positive *thunk*.

Walleye pro Ted Takasaki takes big Lake Erie walleyes on jumbo jigs.

"I jig in kind of a rhythm. If I'm using two rods, I drop one, *thunk*; and then I drop the other one, *thunk*. I just go back and forth. Sometimes you can't keep the fish off the hooks."

You either feel the walleye inhale the jig on the fall, or you feel the weight of the fish when you pick up the jig. Respond with a timely hook set and the walleye should be yours. Although Takasaki has not used jumbo jigging in Lake Erie in the summer and fall, he believes it will work anytime walleyes relate to deep structure.

"It's simply an effective way of presenting live bait in deep water," he says.

Takasaki's reasoning is right on the money, especially in late fall, when walleyes gather in the island area of the western basin prior to ice-up. Jigging in depths to 40 feet or more can dredge up limits of heavyweight walleyes, using the same tactics Takasaki and Demeter rely on in the spring for post-spawn females.

Chapter 6

Weight-Forward Spinners

FISHING WEIGHT-FORWARD spinners rates high with Lake Erie walleye anglers, partly because the method keeps you in touch with the essence of fishing. It's a treat for the senses. You drift quietly, pushed along by the wind and waves. No droning motor dulls the sounds of nature and the voices of your fishing partners. You enjoy the pleasure of casting; the challenge of working a lure. Top it off with that electric moment when you feel the strike, followed by the throbbing weight of a walleye.

WEIGHT-FORWARD CONSTRUCTION

The Erie Dearie has long been synonymous with Lake Erie walleye fishing. Introduced in the late 1960s, this weight-forward spinner has probably accounted for more western basin walleyes than any other lure. Today, you have many brands of capable weight-forward spinners from which to choose.

All weight-forward spinners employ the same basic design, which places the lure's weight ahead of its spinner blade. A short, wire leader attaches

Another Lake Erie walleye succumbs to a weight-forward spinner.

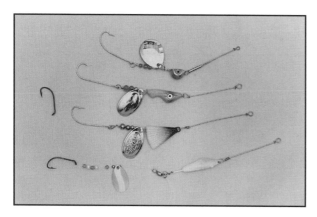

*From top: Hildebrandt's Erie
Shiner; Erie Dearie; Fofrich's
Old Clay Face; Flip 'N Harness.*

to the head of a molded, lead body. The blade spins on a clevis directly behind the body, followed by one or more beads and a free-swinging hook. Tie your line to the wire leader, gob a night crawler on the hook and you're ready to rumble.

Capt. Jim Fofrich has been part of the evolution of weight-forward spinners. A revered western and central basin walleye guide, many of Fofrich's peers regard him as a local angling historian and an unofficial poet laureate for Lake Erie.

"If there's anything better than Lake Erie," he says with passion, "God kept it for himself. She's my gal. I'll never leave her."

Fofrich started fishing Lake Erie in the '40s with his father. By the mid-50s, he was running his own boat and flinging an early weight-forward spinner made by Arbogast called the Paul Bunyan.

"The weight-forward spinner was basically a structure lure back then," says Fofrich. "We'd drift over reefs and swim the lure over the rocks. It wasn't until 1975 that we began fishing weigh-forward spinners in open water away from structure. By 1977, that tactic was in full bloom."

THE COUNT-DOWN METHOD

The discovery that Lake Erie walleye suspend and feed in open water brought about the count-down method which has ruled here for the past two decades. In murky, pre-zebra days, it was common to catch walleyes with weight-forward spinners from just under the surface to the bottom, especially in the western basin.

Walleyes occasionally feed near the surface today, but they usually don't come up as high now that the water is clearer. Even so, weight-forward spinners regularly take fish well above the bottom.

The productive depth may change from hour to hour. It depends on the mood of the walleyes, time of day, weather conditions, water color and the depth of the bait fish. The count-down method lets you determine how deep walleyes are feeding and helps you present a weight-forward spinner at that magic depth cast after cast.

First, cast perpendicular to the boat's drift or downwind. This lets the lure sink freely. If you cast upwind, the drifting boat drags the lure and prevents it from getting down.

If your depthfinder shows fish suspended at a particular depth, say at 20 feet, consider letting the lure sink while you mentally count off 20 seconds. That should put you in the ball park. (The exact sink rate varies, depending on the line's diameter and the lure's weight and design.) Then engage the reel, pull the lure ahead to start the blade spinning and try to maintain a retrieve that keeps the lure swimming at the same depth.

Should several casts at a given count fail to get results, shorten or lengthen the count by 5-second increments to reach different depths. You also may wish to start with a five or 10 count and work your way down, or count the lure to the bottom and work up.

Walleyes sometimes feed so close to the surface that most anglers fish beneath them. In this instance, you must start retrieving the moment the lure hits the water. Charter captains call this "fishing the splash."

When fishing with a party of anglers, such as on a charter, have each person start with a different count. This speeds up the fish-finding process by covering several depths at once. When one angler begins catching fish, the others should duplicate the

FLIP 'N HARNESS

When walleye get finicky, claims Capt. Fofrich, they reject weight-forward spinners before you can set the hook. On days like this, Fofrich puts fish in the cooler by switching to his Flip 'N Harness.

The minnow head on this rig comes in 3/4- and 1-ounce sizes and has a short wire leader typical of weight-forward spinners. The trailing end of the weight, however, pulls a 20-inch monofilament leader that ends in a crawler harness with a single spinner. Fofrich casts the rig with spinning tackle and fishes it just as he does a weight-forward spinner.

"Walleyes," says Fofrich, "usually come up from behind or underneath a lure and knock it forward. With the Flip 'N Harness, the mono lead goes slack and they never feel any resistance. They just pick up the crawler and go with it."

productive retrieve by using the same lure and count.

THE SWING

Fishing the swing goes hand in hand with the countdown method. The swing describes the lures's path during the retrieve.

As we've already discussed, you cast perpendicular to the boat's drift, count the weight-forward spinner down and start the retrieve. The boat keeps drifting throughout this process and soon begins pulling the lure. Slow retrieves usually work better. At times, you may have to stop cranking altogether to prevent the lure from rising. The most common mistake made when fishing the swing is retrieving too fast. Slow down!

Eventually, the weight-forward spinner swings around to the point where it drags directly behind

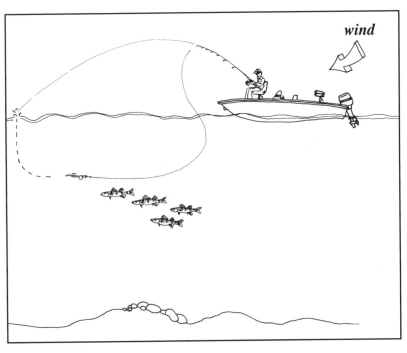

Mentally count weight-forward spinners down to the depth at which suspended walleyes are feeding.

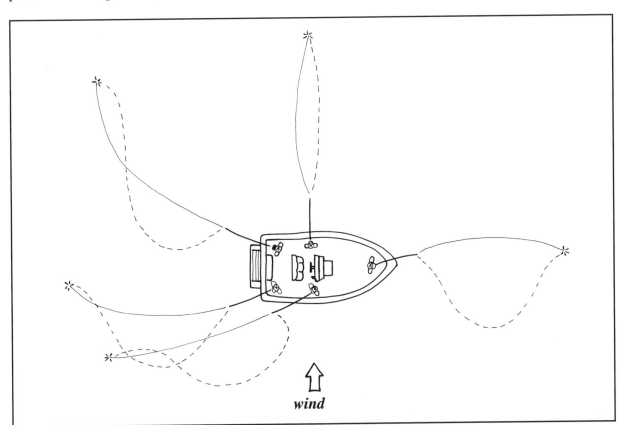

To fish the swing, cast perpendicular to the direction of the drift (see bow and stern anglers above). This ploy lets the lure avoid the pull of the boat throughout most of the retrieve. The downwind cast (top) is also effective for boat-shy fish in clear water.

*Capt. Fofrich fishes the swing
with a weight-forward spinner.*

"The zebras have killed the rock fishing," laments Capt. Dave Demeter. If you told me a dozen years ago that I could hit the Chicks, West Reef and Gull Shoal and not pull a limit of walleyes anytime in July and August, I would have said you were full of it. But you can't pull them on the rock piles anymore."

Walleyes suspended in open water also have grown elusive. They now shy from boats and tend to hold deeper, which makes them more susceptible to trolling. Though the T-Word offends many anglers, trolling can't be beat for sheer efficiency. Even charter captains who dote on weight-forward spinners, including Demeter and Fofrich, have adopted the latest trolling methods.

"My favorite way to fish walleyes," says Fofrich, "is to cast for them. My

the boat. Many strikes occur just as the lure turns in and speeds up. This point marks the end of the swing. As you crank in to make another cast, pause a few times and let the lure drop back. This often triggers strikes from walleyes that are following.

Throughout the retrieve, hold the rod tip low and point it off to the side of the lure. This reduces line bagging caused by the wind and helps you feel strikes.

When several anglers fish from the same boat, casting must be synchronized so everyone may effectively fish the swing. Many boats drift broadside to the wind, which makes the bow and the corners of the transom ideal locations for perpendicular casts. Anglers sandwiched in the middle must cast over the lines of the anglers who hold the prime outside positions. This may be done easily if anglers alternate their casts.

Fishing weight-forward spinners is an inexact science. Not everyone counts with precisely the same cadence or retrieves at the same speed. But anglers who master this method catch walleyes consistently spring through fall.

Before the zebra mussel invasion, even sloppy presentations with weight-forward spinners produced plenty of walleyes. The fish were remarkably tolerant in the murky water. Packs of boats could repeatedly drift over them at midday, and anglers caught them making short casts.

CLEAR WATER REFINEMENTS

There still are times when fishing with weight-forward spinners is sinfully easy, especially on dark days and after wind and waves have roiled the water. But for the most part, the increased water clarity dictates more refined presentations.

*Capt. Fofrich with proof that weight-forward
spinners still catch walleyes on Lake Erie.*

least favorite way is to not catch them at all. I'll do anything to insure that my clients catch fish, even troll."

Like many other reputable captains, Fofrich now has a complete ensemble of trolling gear. He employs it with skill, but only when he has to. That amounts to one day of trolling for every 10 to 15 days of drifting and casting.

"Regardless of the clear water," says Fofrich, "you can catch walleyes with weight-forward spinners on most days. In the summer, I sometimes catch them 55 to 60 feet deep in the central basin with weight-forward spinners."

LURE SELECTION

Before zebra mussels, you rarely needed a weight-forward spinner heavier than 1/2 ounce. Most walleyes were taken on these lures from about 4 to 25 feet deep. While weight-forward spinners in the 1/4- to 1/2-ounce range are still essential when

Anglers aboard a charter boat spread out so they may fish the swing from different positions.

walleyes feed in the upper levels, you also need heavier models. Anglers usually deploy 5/8-ounce to 1-ounce sizes in the 25- to 45-foot depth range. These lures also take fish deeper, as Fofrich attests.

Also bear in mind that thin weight-forward spinners sink faster than those sporting bulging bodies. Many light 1/4-ounce models, for example, feature round bodies that help them ride higher in the water. One of the better deep-water models, Jim Fofrich's Old Clay Face, has a narrow body that slices deep fast.

"I call it the Old Clay Face," says Fofrich, "because it gets right near the bottom. I picked up the name from Gary Roach, one of the best walleye anglers to ever wet a line. He always says, 'let's go out and get a big guy, one with an old clay face.' He's referring to the big walleyes we've caught that have bottom muck on their jaws."

WEIGHT-FORWARD TACKLE

Tackle considerations have grown more discriminating in Lake Erie's clear water. Now you must cast weight-forward spinners as far as possible to reach boat-shy walleyes. Longer rods, such as 6 1/2-foot spinning or baitcasting outfits, launch these lures like rockets. Spinning is generally more popular, but many experienced charter captains opt for baitcasting.

"I lean real heavy on baitcasting," says Fofrich. "On rough seas, I can control a big fish a lot better with baitcasting tackle than I can with spinning gear."

Fofrich carries two custom rods for weight-forward spinners made from 6 1/2-foot Loomis IMX graphite blanks. A medium-heavy rod handles 3/4- to 1-ounce lures; a slightly lighter rod casts 1/2- and 5/8-ounce sizes. The rods have ample backbone for distance casting and hook setting. The sensitive graphite blanks help detect light bites in deep water.

Fofrich fills his reels with 8-pound test monofilament. This line size holds up well, yet is thin enough to cast well and allow for a fast sink rate.

CASTING DOWNWIND

Traditionally, the worst position for casting a weight-forward spinner is from the downwind side of a drifting boat. Many anglers who learned the basics of drift fishing before the zebra mussel invasion avoid this spot as though it were a deadly virus. Here again, clear water has changed how we fish for walleyes in Lake Erie. Now the downwind side gets high marks.

"I try to get three people casting downwind," says Fofrich. "That way, they get their lures in front of the walleyes before the boat runs over the fish and spooks them off to the sides."

Capt. Eddy Abel, who docks his Tight-Liner at Spitzer Lakeside Marine in Lorain, Ohio, usually fishes the lee side of the boat, because his clients prefer other positions. He casts straight downwind and retrieves while the boat moves toward the incoming lure.

"Most of my clients," says Abel, "are amazed at how many fish I pull off that side of the boat. But

HIGH-VIS LINE

"I'm a great believer in watching your line," says Capt. Fofrich. "There are times when you'll see hits before you feel them. It permits you to respond quicker to the strike. That's why I use Berkley's XT Solar line which has super visibility. To make sure the walleyes don't see it, I tie on a 10-foot, clear monofilament leader with a blood knot."

you've got to remember, I'm drifting into the fish. They haven't seen the boat yet. I'm pulling fish at, say, a 15 to 20 count in 60 feet of water, while the guys fishing the swing might have to go with a 25 to 35 count. The boat spooks the high fish out of their reach."

Back in the days of murky water, it was common to catch Lake Erie walleyes that were suspended near the surface by dragging weight-forward spinners behind the boat. Kiss those days goodbye. Also forget about heading into a pack of boats and repeatedly drifting over the same school of walleyes. Lake Erie's clear water put an end to these practices.

The most successful drift fishermen these days steer away from other boats, which is what Capt. Demeter did when I joined him and a group of anglers from Wisconsin during an outing in July. He piloted his 30-foot cruiser, Double D, far out into the western basin from Catawba Island as the rising sun brightened our way. After leaving all but a few other charter boats behind, he set up a drift in a moderate breeze over a bottom that averaged 30 feet deep.

Our boat was one of the first in the area, but others eventually wandered in. Most of them drifted over water we had already covered. Demeter's crew had fished with him before and knew the drill. They took up their favorite casting positions, varied their counts and fished the swing like old hands.

The action wasn't fast, but it was steady. Every 15 minutes or so, another walleye found itself flopping in our cooler. Whenever we hit an occasional dry spell, I expected Demeter to pull around and make another pass over the fish. But he continued the initial drift for more than two hours. By that time many more boats followed in our path. I asked him why he stayed with one drift so long.

"They're touchy now with the clear water," he explained. "We're drifting ahead of the pack and

Capt. Demeter stays away from other boats when drift fishing with weight-forward spinners.

catching walleyes that haven't been bothered. We're netting more fish than the anglers behind us. A pack of boats can drive away a whole school of walleyes. I stay away from other boats whenever I can."

CURSE OF FLAT WATER

Drift fishing requires a breeze to push the boat within casting range of unsuspecting walleyes. Without wind, the boat is dead on the water and, for most people, weight-forward spinners are out.

The curse of flat water doesn't faze Capt. Fofrich. He creates his own drift with an electric motor that is attached to a bracket on the transom. A 28- to 32-pound thrust motor provides more than enough power to push his 27-foot cruiser on calm water.

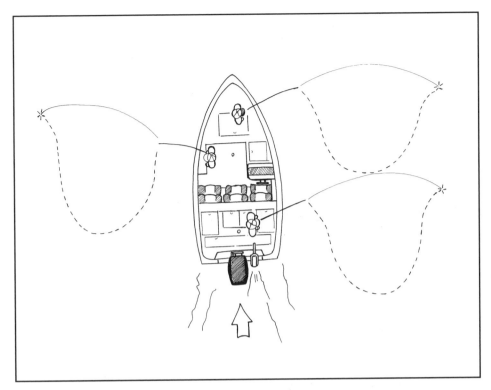

When Lake Erie is flat, Capt. Fofrich creates his own drift with an electric motor. Anglers fish the sweep by casting weight-forward spinners out each side of the boat.

"I call it my Minn Kota breeze," says Fofrich. "I just sit back there and steer the boat with it. My clients cast perpendicular to the boat, three on each side. It's a beautiful swing everybody catches fish."

BAITING UP

Bring plenty of fresh night crawlers when fishing with weight-forward spinners. Before you begin casting, drop a handful of crawlers in a small bucket of ice water. This cleans them off, plumps them up and makes them lively. It keeps the boat cleaner, too. Most anglers gob a whole crawler onto the hook. Not Capt. Fofrich.

"Many times a guy puts a weight-forward spinner in the water without any bait on it to check its action," says Fofrich. "Then he puts a big night crawler on it which just kills the lure's action. You're better off with just a portion of a worm. Maybe just a third of a big worm or a half of a regular worm."

Fofrich believes that there's no substitute for fresh bait. He recommends changing bait regularly, including every time you catch a fish of any kind.

"The odor of that night crawler is a real attractor to those walleyes. If you fish for 15 minutes and don't get a hit, strip the hook and change your bait. Many times you'll generate a hit just by putting on fresh bait."

Chapter 7

Bottom Bouncers

BOTTOM BOUNCING is blue-collar walleye fishing. It doesn't put on airs and performs a workmanlike job of catching Lake Erie walleye under a variety of conditions.

Few anglers know the fine points of bottom bouncing as well as Mike McClelland of Pierre, South Dakota, one of the most successful anglers in the history of professional walleye tournaments. Bottom bouncers have played a major role in his success, which includes many fruitful visits to Lake Erie.

"Even before I fished Lake Erie," says McClelland, "simple arithmetic told me that bottom bouncers would be deadly here. Spinners and crawlers have worked for years on Lake Erie in the form of weight-forward spinners. A boat pulling a bottom bouncer runs a spinner and crawler in productive water 100 percent of the time, compared to 30 percent of the time while casting a weight-forward spinner."

ANATOMY OF A BOTTOM BOUNCER

A bottom bouncer is a length of wire bent into an inverted "L." The short, upper prong measures about 4 inches long. The drop-prong hangs down about 12 inches and has a lead weight molded to it at the midpoint. The weight typically weighs from 1/2 ounce to 3 ounces.

McClelland drags bottom bouncers with 10- or 12-pound monofilament. He generally matches them with spinner rigs tied with 10- to 14-pound test mono, but goes as light as 6-pound test when fishing live bait with a bare hook.

"My leaders are as long as I can spread my arms apart," he laughs. "About 5 1/2 feet."

LIGHT-BITE SYSTEM

McClelland often rigs a modified bottom bouncer, consisting of only the longer wire prong with the weight. He fastens it to the line with a nylon snap made by Quick-Change Systems. The Quick-Change snap slides on the line, but stops

A bottom bouncer holds live bait and spinner rigs up off the bottom.

Mike McClelland with a Lake Erie walleye taken on a bottom bouncer and a spinner rig. Perry's Monument in the background juts up from South Bass Island.

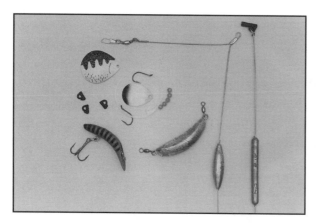

From right: Light Bite with Quick-Change snap; Dakota Bouncer; keel weight; spinner rig with Quick-Change snap; F7 Flatfish.

Mike McClelland changes blades on a spinner rig.

when it reaches the 2-way swivel that connects the line to the leader.

"The Light-bite system allows the line to move freely through the Quick-Change snap," explains McClelland. "When walleyes are hitting short, as they do a lot of times with a crawler on a hook, you can drop your rod tip and feed them line before striking."

Another advantage with the Quick-Change snap is that you may easily switch weights without cutting lines and retying knots. This lets you quickly increase or decrease the weight to match changing conditions.

BASIC BOTTOM BOUNCING

Drag a bottom bouncer across the bottom while drifting or slow trolling with an electric or gas motor. The long wire "bounces" the bottom and holds your offering up where a walleye can see and capture it.

These devices also keep you in touch with bottom changes and drastically reduce snags. A bottom bouncer easily walks over jagged Lake Erie reefs that quickly claim other sinkers.

"A bottom bouncer," says McClelland, "presents a bait a foot off the bottom in any condition, at any depth, with a current, without a current, and even on structures that rise and fall quickly.

"It's very forgiving. If you accidentally slip into water that's deeper or shallower than you intended to fish, the bottom bouncer stays in contact with the bottom and continues to make an effective presentation."

THE GOLDEN RULE

McClelland's essential rule for bottom bouncing is: "Thou shalt let out enough line to reach bottom and maintain a 45 degree angle."

To follow McClelland's Golden Rule, you must select the right weight for the depth you are fishing and drag the bottom bouncer at an appropriate speed. If the speed is too fast or the weight too light, the bottom bouncer trails too far behind

Spinner rigs are becoming more popular on Lake Erie.

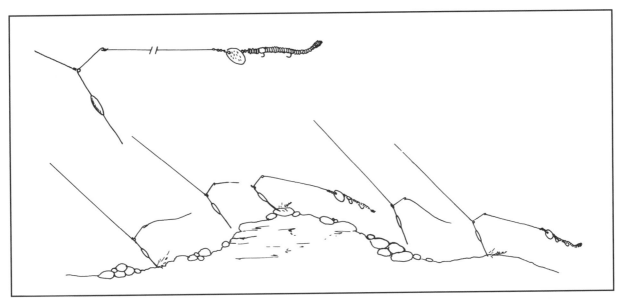

McClelland keeps track of lake Erie's reefs by working a bottom bouncer with a lift-drop motion.

the boat. Instead of walking tall, it falls over and loses its advantage. If the weight is too heavy or the speed too slow, the bottom bouncer walks too close to the boat, which also hinders its effectiveness.

BOUNCING REEFS

"If you fish Lake Erie's reefs with bottom bouncers during the spawn and right afterward," says McClelland, "you'll catch so many male walleyes that it's more work than fun. They aren't the biggest walleyes in the lake, but you'll catch all the 2- to 5-pound fillet fish you want."

Before he fishes, McClelland zigzags over the edges of a reef, looking for concentrations of walleyes with his Lowrance LMS 350 liquid crystal graph. He admits that the fishing is sometimes so good on the reefs that you may fish these structures randomly and catch plenty of walleyes. But when the bite is tough, more precise presentations are necessary.

The fish may cluster on the top of a reef, on the crown of a drop-off, the bottom of a drop-off or half way up a drop. Once he determines the depth and location that holds the greatest concentration of fish, McClelland keys on that area. When fishing Erie's reefs, he rarely probes water deeper than about 22 feet or goes with bottom bouncers weighing more than 1 1/2 ounce.

"On the reefs," he says, "you don't drag a bottom bouncer, you keep track of the bottom. Lift it up, set it down; lift it up, set it down. If you go off of a 6-inch break, you know it, same as you would a jig."

If you don't exercise a lift-drop motion, you lose track of the bottom. An unbroken, steady retrieve also maintains a constant forward pull on the bait, resulting in short strikes. Many of the "pecks" you feel will be walleyes nipping off the tails of your crawlers.

A walleye usually falls in behind the bait and inhales it by flaring its gills and sucking in the water around it. When there is constant pressure from a fishing line, only the lose end of the crawler flows into the fish's mouth. That's why worm harnesses feature multiple hooks. Many walleyes nab only the trailing hook.

"But if you fish a bottom bouncer with the attitude of keeping track of the bottom," says McClelland, "every time you drop the rod tip and touch bottom, the weight stops and creates slack in the leader. That slack lets a walleye deeply inhale the bait."

RODS

When bottom bouncing reefs, McClelland holds one rod in his hand and puts another in a rod holder. The hand-held rod is a 5-foot, 6-inch, Quantum baitcasting outfit made by Daiwa. It features a sensitive, medium-action blank and a short pistol grip. The pistol grip lets McClelland effortlessly point his rod down so the tip nearly touches the water when the bottom bouncer hits bottom. This posture helps him monitor the slightest change in depth.

An 8 1/2-foot Quantum steelhead rod rests in a holder parallel to the water. When waves rock the boat, the rod lifts and drops, causing the bottom bouncer to play tag with the bottom. The long rod prevents tangled lines. Its slow, fiberglass blank bows deeply when a walleye bites, affording an excellent visual strike indicator.

Walleye Pro Mark Brumbaugh taps a reef with a bottom bouncer while watching a rod in a holder.

"I have tunnel vision on the rod in my hand," says McClelland. "The rod in the holder is a bonus rod, but sometimes it outfishes the rod I'm holding."

DROP WEIGHTS FOR DEEP WATER

Pulling spinner rigs with drop weights in Erie's open water produces many heavy-weight walleyes for McClelland. For this application, he puts all the rods in holders, including his partner's.

McClelland relies on a Quick Change snap, but replaces the Light Bite wire form with a length of monofilament attached to a drop weight. This setup may be used in deep water, since snagging isn't a problem on Erie's flat, mud bottoms.

"Your best chance for catching big fish at Erie," says McClelland, "is generally on the bottom. So I always keep a couple of lines set right on the bottom or a foot up. I experiment with the other rods."

A typical bottom setup for McClelland would be a 3-ounce drop weight on a 1-foot lead, a combination that drags bottom 50 feet deep. If he's marking walleyes 3 or 4 feet above bottom, he goes with a 5 foot lead. This lets him maintain bottom contact, yet still reach the fish.

"For suspended fish," says McClelland, "I switch to weights as light as 1/2-ounce, which puts me up around 17 feet. With four rods pulling 50 feet of line, I can cover four depth ranges by running four different weights.

"If I hit a fish on the half-ounce weight, I'll rig another rod with it. If I hit another on that size weight, I'll raise everything up."

SPINNER RIGS

When pulling spinner rigs behind drop weights, McClelland opts for worm harness that bear two No. 6 Excalibur treble hooks spaced 4 inches apart. When dragging bottom bouncers on Erie's snag-infested reefs, his spinner rigs have two No. 4 single hooks.

A basic rule of thumb is to use a large blade—up to a No. 7 Indiana or Colorado—when fishing deep or in murky water. Smaller blades are often more effective in clear water and on the reefs.

Be sure enough beads separate the blade from the leading hook. When lying

When dragging drop weights over Erie's deep, mud bottoms, McClelland puts all the rods in holders.

flat, the end of the blade should rest about half an inch ahead the hook. If it's too close, the whirling blade prevents walleyes from getting hooked.

"Sometimes there's no rhyme or reason why walleyes prefer certain blades," admits McClelland. "You just keep experimenting with sizes and colors until you find what they want through trial and error."

The same company that makes plastic snaps for attaching bottom bouncers to the line, Quick Change Systems, also manufactures quick release clevises for blades. "They makes changing blades a snap," says McClelland.

The most common mistake anglers make with spinner rigs, McClelland has found, is not moving fast enough to make the blades spin. He always drops the rig into the water next to the boat to make sure the drifting or trolling speed is sufficient to turn the blade.

"If you're not moving fast enough to spin the blade," he says, "you have to increase your speed or go up in blade size. Most people go smaller in this situation, but it takes more speed to turn smaller blades."

As for blade colors, McClelland doesn't believe this is as important as most anglers think. He carries every color blade imaginable, but believes this factor is insignificant compared to depth, speed and blade size.

"People spend too much time thinking about colors," says McClelland. "If you and I are fishing and you whack a walleye on white and I'm using orange, I don't change to white. I don't do that until you catch two fish."

Though McClelland doesn't have a color preference, he's a stickler for blades that have nickel backs. He has studied blades in a swimming pool and claims that the brightest flash reflects off the cupped side. The outside of the blade parades its color, while the inside gives off a bright, metallic flash. Because walleyes tend to follow spinners before striking, they see more of the blade's nickel side than its painted side.

LIVE BAIT RIGS

When walleyes demand a subtle presentation, or speeds that are too slow to turn spinners, McClelland rigs up a plain 6-pound leader with a No. 1 or No. 2 light wire Aberdeen hook. He relies mainly on crawlers on Lake Erie, but sometimes goes with a minnows or leeches. He hooks minnows through the lips, crawlers through the middle and leeches near the sucker.

To combat short-striking walleyes, McClelland places a small foam float in the middle of the leader. This lifts the leader slightly above the bait and provides a little slack line that helps walleyes inhale the bait.

Another trick McClelland uses—which accomplishes pretty much the same thing—is that of rigging with a coiled leader. This is typically 12-pound monofilament that has taken a set on a reel and coils like a spring. When a walleye takes the bait, the coils provide just enough slack to insure a solid hookup. The drawback with coiled leaders is that you must tie on a new one after catching a fish or snagging bottom, because the coil straightens under the stress.

BOAT CONTROL

McClelland has logged countless miles pulling bottom bouncers with bow-mounted electric motors. This setup is unbeatable for controlling the speed and adroitly following the irregular contours of Lake Erie's reefs. A boat with an electric motor mounted on the transom is not nearly as responsive.

In open water, McClelland cranks up a small auxiliary gas outboard on the transom and sets it at the appropriate speed for pulling drop weights and spinner rigs. He then locks the motor so that it points straight ahead and steers the boat with the wheel on the console. The bigger, primary outboard serves as a rudder.

DRIFTING

Drifting spinner rigs can be effective over reefs and open water, provided the breeze pushes the boat fast enough whirl the blades. Capt. Bob Troxel, of Foxhaven Marina on Catawba Island, Ohio, frequently has employs this tactic. He turns his 30 foot cruiser broadside to the wind and places three or four rods with spinner rigs in holders on the upwind gunnel. Should the breeze really kick up, he slows the boat with a drift sock.

When drifting over reefs, Troxel drags bottom bouncers. In open water, he weights spinners with in-line keel sinkers. Leader lengths vary from as short as 18 inches for aggressive fish to 6 feet when walleyes prove finicky.

When drifting over mud flats in the western basin, Troxel usually finds himself in 30 to 33 feet of water. In a slight breeze, he generally uses a 3/4- or

Capt. Troxel drags spinners behind keel sinkers while drifting with the wind.

1-ounce keel sinker. In a strong wind, he may have to go up to 3 or 4 ounces.

"When I start the drift," says Troxel, "I let out line until the sinker hits bottom. Then I put the rod into an upright holder and take up a crank or two. I try to use a weight that keeps the line at about a 45 degree angle. If I don't do any good with the spinner near the bottom, I'll take it up two or three cranks. I keep doing that until I start hitting fish. Then I set my other rods at that same level."

As the drifting boat pulls the spinner rigs, Troxel's clients cast weight-forward spinners and fish the swing. Some days casting methods prevail. On other days, the drift rods get most of the action.

"Some my best days have come dragging keel sinker rigs," says Troxel. "One day a group of mine caught a limit of walleyes that included 22 weighing from 5 to more than 10 pounds. Every big fish came on a dead stick and a spinner. It seemed like every time you looked, one of those rods was bending over."

Drift fishing with bottom bouncers is nothing new to Capt. Eddy Abel who fishes the central basin out of Spitzer Lakeside Marina in Lorain, Ohio. Abel goes with traditional 3/4- to 1-ounce bottom bouncers when drifting over rocky, near-shore structures. In deeper water, he increases the weight to 1 1/2-ounce or more.

In addition to spinner rigs, Abel takes many walleyes dragging F6 and F7 Flatfish. These small Flatfish sport single treble hooks. Green and chartreuse patterns prevail. Abel tips the hook with a crawler.

"I call them dead rigs," says Abel. "On day with a fairly decent wind, I just put the Flatfish down on long lines and stick the rods in holders. You'd be surprised how many fish they take."

Any angler who has fished bottom bouncers and weighted spinner rigs on Lake Erie has seen these setups haul in plenty of walleyes. They're among the easiest and least expensive means for catching walleyes. Some would say almost foolproof.

"A bottom bouncer isn't magic," says McClelland, "but there are times when it sure seems like it is."

ARTIFICIAL MINNOWS

McClelland's bottom bouncers occasionally tow shallow running minnow baits, such as the Rapala and Rebel Minnow. He especially likes this combination when fishing reefs that have sharp turns. No other trolling technique does a better job of precisely following a twisting contour with a crankbait.

A key time for the long minnow rig when you can't get a bite on a prime bottom structure that is loaded with bait fish. That's when McClelland suspects that complacent walleyes are nearby. He usually finds them on the sharpest drop-off.

"You can drag live bait through them," says McClelland, "and they're not interested. But if you run a big Rebel Minnow in front of them, they'll just wail on it."

Breaking with conventional wisdom, McClelland drags a bottom bouncer and long minnow straight up and down drop-offs, a tactic that finds walleye wherever they're holding. "It's the only way I know of to fish a crankbait a foot off the bottom on that kind of structure," he says.

Chapter 8

Basic Trolling

MANY ANGLERS troll only after walleyes ignore their casting presentations. It's a last resort. Drag lures behind the boat and hope you get lucky. As good as the walleye fishing is on Lake Erie, this approach nets few fish.

Refined trolling methods, on the other hand, are proving deadly and often necessary for walleyes in Lake Erie's clear water. In many instances, you either troll or go without fish.

"Trolling now is a very specialized, scientific method of harvesting fish," says Rick LaCourse, a long-time Lake Erie charter captain who now makes his living fishing professional walleye tournaments. "There are so many variables to consider, it really keeps you on your toes."

DEPTH

The first consideration is: How deep are the fish?

"Locating the fish is the toughest part," says LaCourse. "Once you find them with your electronics, they're going to tell you how deep to troll. It's pure and simple."

If LaCourse marks fish consistently at 18 to 20 feet, for example, he trolls a lure that runs 15 to 16 feet deep. Walleyes readily swim up a few feet to nail a lure, but rarely swim down to do so.

The most basic trolling presentation consists of pulling diving crankbaits on flat lines. A flat line is one that goes from the rod tip to a free-running lure without any weights or trolling devices.

Crankbaits with large diving lips run deeper

Walleye pro Rick LaCourse relies on a liquid crystal graph to locate walleyes on Lake Erie.

Rick LaCourse knows that refined trolling methods consistently take walleyes on Lake Erie, as does Capt. Randy Randebaugh who is handling the net.

When trolled at the right depth, crankbaits are deadly.

The amount of line let out also influences a crankbait's depth. A lure that runs only 10 feet deep on 60 feet of line, may get down 25 feet when let back 200 feet. But there is a point of diminishing returns.

Although trolling speed is another factor, there is little depth variation with crankbaits trolled at the slow to moderate speeds typically used for walleyes. Bear in mind that faster speeds make crankbaits run shallower, which is just the opposite of what most anglers believe.

To achieve a desired trolling depth, you must factor in the lure's design, the line diameter and the length of line let out. How do you figure such an equation with any kind of accuracy? By letting someone else do it. Reference books and charts are available that spell out how deep the most popular crankbaits run with different line sizes and on varying lengths of line.

LaCourse relies on "Crankbaits In-Depth" by Dr. Steven Holt and Tom Irwin. Another publication, "CRANKBAITS, A guide to Casting and Trolling Depths of 200 Popular Lures," was compiled by Mike McClelland of Pierre, South Dakota, a top walleye pro.

These reference guides also apply when trolling crankbaits behind in-line boards and big boards. In fact, all the basic trolling setups discussed in this chapter may be used with boards.

than those with small lips, and larger crankbaits generally run deeper than smaller ones of similar design. Some lure manufacturers list approximate running depths for their crankbaits, but this is only a starting point.

Regardless of the crankbait being used, it cannot achieve its maximum depth unless it runs true. Many crankbaits, even new ones, must be tuned. Perform this chore by swimming a lure alongside a boat running at trolling speed. If the crankbait swims to the left of center, bend the line tie gently to the right with pliers; vice versa if the lure runs to the right of center. Keep checking and making adjustments until the lure runs straight.

Crankbaits dive much deeper when trolled than cast, more than twice as deep in many cases. The lighter the line, the deeper a crankbait dives. A lure that runs 18 feet deep with 12-pound line may dig 24 feet deep with 6-pound line, provided all other factors are equal.

DUPLICATION

The key to success with any trolling method is duplication. When you catch a walleye, duplicating the trolling setup returns your lure to the productive depth. It matters not that you know exactly how deep the lure is running.

Duplication gets tricky when you troll several lures at varying distances behind the boat. How do you keep track of them all? How do you determine how much line you've let out in the first place?

Line counter reels are one solution. As the lure pays out, a counter attached to the top of the reel marks off the distance. Remember the distance and you can duplicate the setting.

A less expensive method is to determine how much line peels off a standard trolling reel each time the level wind guide makes one pass across the spool.

*A small rubber band serves
as a cheap line counter.*

end of the rubber band through the other and pull it snug to the line.

When you reel in a walleye or check a lure, the rubber band winds onto the spool. If you want to set the lure back the same distance, feed out line until the rubber band winds off the spool. Presto! You have exactly duplicated the trolling distance without remembering a thing. How smart of you.

WEIGHT-ASSISTED TROLLING

Adding weight to the line gets crankbaits deeper and makes other lures, such as spinner rigs, effective for trolling in deep water. Speed duplication becomes more critical with weight-assisted trolling. Slow speeds allow weights to pull lures deeper, while faster speeds swing lures closer to the surface. Even slight speed variations cause substantial depth changes.

KEEL WEIGHTS

Placing a keel sinker ahead of the lure provides a simple and effective means for getting deeper. A bead chain extending from each end of the sinker prevents line twist. Attach the rod line to one end of the bead chain; the leader to the other end. The leader must be shorter than the rod so you may reel fish close enough to net them.

Some anglers claim that keel sinkers and short leaders put off finicky fish and hinders lure action, especially with crankbaits. Accomplished trollers believe longer leaders and less noticeable weight systems account for more walleyes.

LEAD-CORE

When renowned Wisconsin walleye pros Gary Parsons and Keith Kavajecz first visited Lake Erie, they scored well on walleyes by trolling long minnows with lead-core line. Lead-core is a Dacron line encasing a lead filler. The Dacron provides the strength; the lead filler the weight. To help you keep track of how much line is out, the lead-core is a different color every 10 yards.

This may be done on land by pulling out line and measuring it. One popular reel, for example, lets out approximately 10 feet of line for every pass of the level wind guide. Setting a lure back 100 feet with this reel requires 10 passes. By remembering the number of passes, you can duplicate the trolling setup with reasonable accuracy.

You say your memory isn't everything you hoped it would be? Don't sweat it. A inexpensive trick with a rubber band will make you look like a genius.

First let the lure back as far as you wish, engage the spool and place the rod in a holder. Then take a little No. 8 rubber band (bring a bag of them with you) and fold it around the line just above the reel. Pass one

Three colors (or 90 feet of 18- to 36-pound lead-core) covers the most common trolling depths for Lake Erie walleye, although shorter sections of lead-core may be used as conditions warrant. Monofilament leaders up to 50 feet in length let lures swim with an unrestricted action. Leaders as short as 3 feet deliver more precise lure placement when walleyes hold tight to bottom structures. Use 8- to 10-pound monofilament for leaders and 10- to 12-pound test for backing.

Connect monofilament line to lead-core with a No. 14 crane swivel. Peel back a few inches of the Dacron sheathing and trim a strand of the exposed lead before tying the knot. Dab Super Glue on the knot to keep it from unraveling.

DEPTH REFERENCES

"Crankbaits In-Depth," a laminated book by Dr. Steven Holt and Tom Irwin, may be ordered by sending $22.95 (shipping included) to Sportsman's Corner Publishing, 2304 Olthoff Dr., Muskegon, MI 49444. For credit card orders call: 1-800-353-6958.

Mike McClelland's book, "CRANK-BAITS, A Guide to Casting & Trolling Depths of 200 Popular Lures," may be purchased from Fishing Enterprises, 800 S. Washington, P.O. Box 7108, Pierre, SD 57501. Phone: (605) 223-9126. The price at this writing is $11.95, plus $2 for shipping and handling. The "Crankbait Trolling Depth Guide and Calculator" may be ordered from the same address for $9.95, plus $2 for shipping and handling. The calculator is laminated.

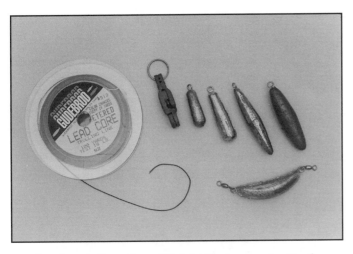

Lead-core line, Snap Weight System and a Keel sinker, three means of weight-assisted trolling.

SNAP WEIGHTS

The Snap Weight System consists of line releases that connect to lead sinkers weighing from 1/2 to 8 ounces. A Snap Weight is usually fastened to a line well in front of a lure, typically 20 to 100 feet. The rule of thumb is: the clearer the water, the longer the lead.

Simply let the lure out behind a moving boat an appropriate distance and snap on the weight. Then let out more line to achieve the desired depth. When reeling in a walleye or the lure, pause briefly as the weight nears the rod tip and snap it off.

"With this system," says Parsons, "I don't have to have separate reels set up with lead-core. All I need is a little tackle box filled with Snap Weights."

After attaching a Snap Weight, Parsons determines the depth by maintaining a specific trolling speed and letting out line until he feels bottom. He then notes the setting on his line counter reel.

"If the reel reads 200 feet," says Parsons, "and it's 50 feet deep, I know that I have to let out half that much line (100 feet) to reach 25 feet. That gives me an approximate range. I'll start going up and down from there, until I start getting bites. From then on, it's a matter of duplication."

An alternative method of finding a productive depth is to set out several identical lines and lures, but with Snap Weights in different sizes. This covers a range of depths and lets the walleyes tell you which they prefer.

Snap Weights work especially well on Lake Erie when matched with crankbaits and spinner rigs. Spinner rigs trolled behind Snap Weights are likely to produce Lake Erie walleye spring through fall. The

While trolling slowly between .5 to 1.5 m.p.h., let out enough line for the lure to hit bottom. Then reel in until the lure swims freely.

A 6 1/2-foot, long-handled rod with a stiff butt serves well. Place the rod in a holder, pointing straight out from the gunnel and parallel to the water. This reduces line whipping on rough water and produces a more obvious bow when a walleye strikes.

If you're not getting results near the bottom, bring the lure up, taking note of how many times you turn the reel handle. Continue this until a walleye pops the lure. Then return to the same trolling speed and crank the lure up from the bottom the same number of revolutions. This puts your lure right back in the productive depth range.

Though lead-core is effective, Parsons now prefers the Snap Weight System from Off Shore Tackle.

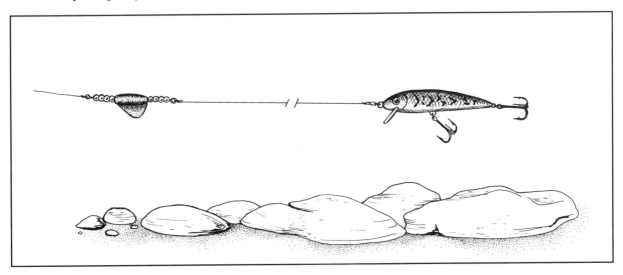

A keel weight is a simple and effective device for trolling lures deeper.

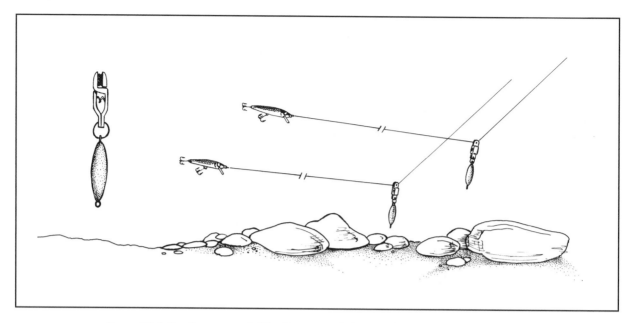

Snap Weights let you quickly change weights to alter the trolling depth.

Rapala, Bomber Long A, Storm ThunderStick and other shallow running minnow lures perform best when the water is 50 degrees or colder.

As the water warms, diving crankbaits come into their own. Some of the more popular models in Lake Erie include Storm's diving ThunderStick Jr. and Hot 'N' Tot, Bomber's 9A, 24A and 25A, Luhr Jensen's Power Dive Minnow, Rapala's Shad Rap and Reef Runner's deep diving Ripstick.

Hangups are rare when trolling over Lake Erie's deep, mud bottoms. But to prevent snags from stealing your Snap Weights, attach them to the releases with snap swivels. First clamp the release to your line. Then open the snap that holds the weight and close it around the line. When reeling in a walleye, free the release and let the weight slide down the line to the lure.

A small rubber band provides another means of attaching a weight to a line. Run the rubber band through the eye of the weight and loop one end over the other. Then fold the rubber band around the line and slip the weight through the opposing loop. This setup is less costly should it break off. When cranking up a walleye, grasp the weight and jerk it down to break the rubber band.

WIRE LINE

Art Lyon of Conneaut, Ohio, helped popularize wire line trolling in the central basin. He favors 10- or 12-pound test, single strand, Williams or American brand wire line. By trolling wire line without weights or other devices, Lyon easily drags bottom with a Rat-L-Trap 25 feet deep. A Norman Deep N digs down 60 feet when pulled by 100 yards of wire line, and other diving plugs get down more than 70 feet deep.

Wire line must be handled carefully to avoid kinks which severely weaken it. Lyon uses only trolling reels that have fairly large spool diameters

Crankbaits run deep when trolled with single strand, wire line.

*A wireless temperature and speed
probe attaches to a downrigger ball.*

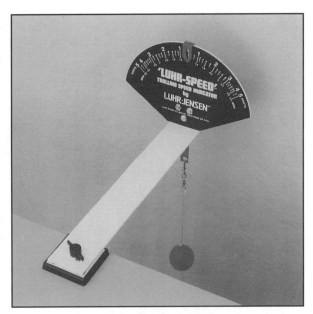

*Luhr Jensen's Luhr-Speed
trolling speed indicator.*

capable of holding at least 200 yards of line. Since wire line has no stretch, he sets his drags light to prevent the hooks from ripping free. He also employs long, limber trolling rods that cushion the strike and the ensuing battle, such as 7- to 8-foot fiberglass downrigger rods with ceramic guides. The wire line grooves the guides, but the grooves don't damage the line.

Attach the wire directly to a plug with the Haywire Twist. Run the wire through the split ring or a snap swivel, cross it back over itself and make about eight tight twists. Wrap the tag end of the wire a few more times and trim the excess close.

SPEED CONTROL

Speed control is nearly as important as depth control. You may pull lures past scads of walleyes, but if the trolling speed is too fast or slow, your offerings will be ignored.

Productive trolling speeds for Lake Erie range from roughly .5 to 3 m.p.h. Generally, you troll slower in cold water and faster in warm water. The exact speed is often critical. Sometimes a speed change of just .1 m.p.h. means the difference between getting few bites and catching limits of heavy fish.

Once you've found a productive trolling speed, it behooves you to stay with it. That sounds simple,

but maintaining a specific speed is impossible without some type of gauge. Many anglers rely on their tachometers, which is misleading. With the engine running at the same speed, a boat trolls faster going with the waves than against them.

Those who own a Loran or GPS system may refer to the speed over ground (SOG) readout. While helpful, this is far from exact. Speedometers that come with some LCGs provide a fair indication, but their paddle wheel sensors are subject to surface water currents.

A more accurate device is something along the lines of Luhr Jensen's Luhr-Speed indicator. This simple unit mounts to the boat's gunnel and drops a sensor (a weight on a line) below the surface where it is less affected by wind or water action. The forward movement of the boat makes the weight swing back, which tilts the mechanical indicator on the gauge. It reveals trolling speeds in 1/10 increments from 0 to 5 knots.

Some of the most accomplished trollers on Lake Erie rely on a wireless temperature and speed probe that attaches to a downrigger ball, such as the one made by Fish Hawk. It sends signals to a gauge on the console that reveals the temperature and the speed of the lures at the actual trolling depth. Charter captain Andy Emrisko, who runs his Wave Walker out of Cleveland Lakefront State Park, adjusts his trolling speed according to the probe.

"Speed is critical," emphasizes Emrisko. "That deep probe is costly, but it's worth it.

"Underwater currents determine the true trolling speed of a lure. The boat's speed on the surface may

Gary Parsons uses line counter reels to help him duplicate successful trolling setups.

the drag slips. The spool should be large enough to hold at least 200 yards of 20-pound test monofilament.

Line counter reels, such as Daiwa's SG27LC, simplify the task of duplicating trolling patterns. Several less costly level wind models also do nicely, such as Penn's 309M.

Match the reels with medium to medium-heavy action trolling rods 7-feet or more in length. The tip should be limber enough to telegraph strikes, yet the butt must have enough backbone to withstand the heavy drag caused by a big, deep diving crankbait. Graphite isn't necessary, since you normally see the strikes while the rods rest in holders. Fiberglass rods and composite rods of fiberglass and graphite perform nicely for most trolling tasks.

ROD HOLDERS

There is no need to hold a rod with most trolling applications. Placing rods in holders eliminates fatigue and lets you take advantage of the two lines you are allotted in U.S waters.

be over a mile an hour faster or slower than the lure being trolled in deep water."

Many boats have trouble trolling at speeds under 2 m.p.h., which are often required for walleyes on Lake Erie. A small, auxiliary outboard provides an excellent means for slowing down. If that's not an option, put out trolling socks on each side of the boat. These are essentially sea anchors that catch the water when the boat moves ahead and slow forward progress.

Another remedy is a mechanical device that fastens to the primary motor's cavitation plate just above the propeller. The Fish-On Troller by Tempress, the Hydro Troll, and the Happy Troll are examples. When the metal flap extends straight back, it works as a trim tab to help the boat up on plane. For trolling, the flap folds down behind the prop, reducing its thrust. This lets you achieve slower trolling speeds without the expense of a smaller motor.

RODS AND REELS

Workhorse reels for trolling on Lake Erie include level wind models that feature low gear ratios from 3:1 to 4.2:1. They stand up to the rigors of trolling and reduce the effort required to wind in lures that cause heavy resistance. Unlike spinning reels, level wind reels do not twist the line, even when

For most trolling applications, rods should be placed in holders.

Permanent and removable rod holders attach to transoms and gunnels. Some holders remain fixed in one position, while others may be set at different angles. Adjustable models help spread lines and let you employ a variety of trolling tactics.

When using rod holders, you detect most strikes by watching the rod tips. Seeing strikes is much easier when two or more rods rest side by side, because their tips dance in sync until a walleye attacks. Sometimes the assault makes the rod tip rattle sharply up and down. In many instances, the rod merely takes a deeper bow than others.

The moment you see that a walleye is on, snatch the rod from it's holder and maintain steady pressure as you reel the fish in. *Don't set the hook!* The boat's forward movement has already embedded the hook for you. Jerking back on the rod may rip the hooks free.

Capt. Jerry Lee lets an autopilot steer the boat when trolling so he can tend the lines.

LURE ACTION

Flat water rarely occurs on the open expanses of Lake Erie. On most days a prevailing breeze pushes waves that lift and shove the boat. The movement transfers to the rods in their holders and on down to the lines, causing lures to race and stall erratically. This type of action helps coax strikes from walleyes.

There are times, however, when it pays to pull a rod from its holder and pump it to impart more action to the lure. This trick may turn things around anytime walleyes refuse to bite, especially on calm days. Gary Parsons, one of the most respected walleye pros in the country, learned this tactic from his father and uses it often.

"Walleyes frequently follow lures without biting," says Parsons. "Pumping the rod alters the lure's action and triggers a strike.

"I drop the rod back to the 8 o'clock position and hold it for a few seconds. Then I very slowly pull it up to about 10 o'clock and hold it briefly. I get a lot of strikes right then, but most strike take place when I return the rod slowly back to 8 o'clock. The lure slows down right in the walleye's face. That often proves irresistible."

Pump the rod with slow movements that maintain constant line tension. You should feel the lure working at all times, as well as the sudden *tick* when a walleye strikes. This is one instance when you should set the hook while trolling. Just don't get carried away. Simply sweep the rod tip back firmly and the walleye should be yours.

AUTOPILOT

When trolling with multiple rods, the boat must continue moving ahead until all the lines are brought in. Turn too sharply while trolling, or let the boat stop and drift, and you invite an impossible nest of tangled lines.

Anyone who trolls Lake Erie should seriously consider installing an autopilot. This device automatically steers the boat on a set course, allowing you to tend rods and land fish without interruption. Experienced Lake Erie charter captains who rely on autopilots efficiently manage a dozen trolling rods at a time with few line problems.

Even a pair of anglers trolling only four lines can get into trouble without an autopilot. All it takes is for two or more walleyes to hook up at the same time, a common occurrence on Lake Erie, and you've got mayhem.

I've fished with several different Lake Erie charter captains who use a variety of capable autopilots. One that especially impresses me is the Benmar Outbound. It features a directional adjustment knob that lets you alter the boat's course without touching the steering wheel.

I watched Captain Jerry Lee operate his Benmar Outbound when we trolled for walleyes in Brest Bay along the Michigan shoreline. He had fixed the autopilot's control unit to the underside of his cruiser's hardtop where he could reach it while standing within easy reach of the rods. We made circular trolling passes in the bay for several hours while fishing among other boats. Lee never once had to enter the cabin to steer the boat. He made all necessary adjustments with the autopilot.

Many of the trolling techniques discussed in this book were developed on other walleye waters or adapted from salmon and lake trout techniques. These methods continue to be, fine-tuned for Lake Erie's walleye. One reason they work so well here is due to the fishery itself.

Accomplished trollers, such as Capt. Jerry Lee, left, consistently take walleyes from Lake Erie.

"The difference between Erie and other bodies of water," says Parsons, "is that Erie is an easy fishery. Erie is almost like heaven, because you can make so many mistakes and still catch fish. It's incredible."

SUPER TROLLING LINES

Super braided lines made from gel-spun polyethylene fibers have found favor with some Lake Erie trollers. A new breed of super lines made from the same material may become even more prominent. The new lines are not braided. Instead, microfibers are bundled or twisted together lengthwise and fused together.

Berkley's FireLine, SpiderWire's Fusion and Raptor's Thermofused Fishing Line fall into this category. These lines handle more like monofilament and retain advantages found in super braids, such as low stretch, high sensitivity, small diameter, superior strength and no memory. The new lines also reduce problems with knot slippage that plague braided lines.

"This stuff is thin," says walleye pro Gary Parsons. "That's its biggest advantage for trolling. The diameter of 10-pound FireLine is about the same as 4-pound monofilament. This may be one of best trolling lines ever. A bait that normally runs 14 feet deep on monofilament will run 25 feet down with FireLine.

To compensate for the no-stretch characteristic of the super lines, you should employ softer rods and use lighter drag settings. Failing to make these adjustments results in hooks pulling out of the fish.

Chapter 9

Diving Planes

Capt. Bob Troxel's first experience with diving planes illustrates why these trolling devices should be mainstays for every Lake Erie walleye angler. The outing took place on a hot July afternoon several years ago.

Drift fishing with weight-forward spinners had slumped badly after the peak early summer season. Faced with markedly clearer water due to the zebra mussel invasion, Troxel conceded that he would have to adopt trolling methods to catch boat-shy walleyes in deep water.

Heading his 30-foot cruiser, "This Is Reality," out from Foxhaven Marina on Catawba Island, Troxel and two friends boated west of Rattlesnake Island in the western basin. When the graph began marking fish near the bottom in 32 feet of water, they put out four brand new diving planes matched with spoons fresh out of their colorful packages.

"I really didn't know what to expect," says Troxel. "But I didn't have much time to think about it. In two hours we landed three limits of big walleyes, including one over 11 pounds. It was unbelievable."

The relatively low cost of diving planes, plus the fact that other anglers were enjoying excellent results with them, figured into Troxel's decision to try this method of trolling. He still relies on the same brand of diver he started with—Luhr Jensen's Dipsy Diver.

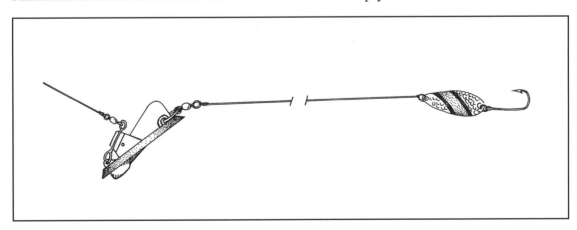

A diving plane followed by a spoon is a deadly combination for big walleyes throughout Lake Erie.

Clockwise from top: Slide Diver; No. 1 Dipsy Diver; No. 0 Dipsy Diver with "O" ring; Kastaway Diver.

ESSENTIAL DIVERS

Available in three sizes that run at depths ranging from 14 to more than 50 feet, the Dipsy Diver is built around a hard plastic disk. The larger two sizes come with an "O" ring that expands their diameters and increases their running depths. These models also feature an adjustable release mechanism that attaches to the rod line. Snap the release in place and the Dipsy digs powerfully downward. When the release breaks free, the Dipsy flattens and stops diving, eliminating its strong resistance.

What makes the Dipsy so versatile is its directional feature. On a 0 setting, the diver runs true. But when an underside weight is adjusted to the right or left of center on specific settings from 1 to 3, the diver angles to the left or right side of the boat. The higher the setting, the farther the diver swings out.

Using different settings spreads the lines, which prevents tangles and increases the width of the trolling swath. Some charter captains set out as many as eight divers at a time. The center divers run deepest, while those set to sweep farthest away from the boat run shallowest.

Another directional diving plane, Kastaway's Diver, features a magnetic release. Should the release inadvertently pop free—a common problem with these types of divers—simply drop the rod tip sharply to put a little slack in the line. This allows the magnetic release to reset itself and averts the chore of winding the diver all the way up. The Kastaway comes in three sizes that dive from 50 to 80 feet

Leaders on most divers must not exceed the rod's length so that fish may be reeled close enough to net them. A short leader helps when trolling spoons, since it gives them a snappier action. Long minnow crankbaits and other lures, however, may trigger more strikes when trolled on longer leaders.

The directional Slide Diver, from U-Charters Inc., overcomes this dilemma. The rod line feeds through the Slide Diver's release mechanism, so you may set the lure back as far as you wish from the diver. When a walleye strikes, the release opens and the diver slides down the line to the fish. Randy Even, who designed the Slide Diver, recommends using an abrasion resistant line, such as 20-pound Berkley XT.

Diving planes are typically set back from the boat 75 to 180 feet. Most divers come with charts that indicate how deep they run at different settings. With 125 feet of line out, for example, the standard Kastaway Diver reaches 55 feet at the 1 (center) setting, 48 feet at the 3 setting and 42 feet at the 5 setting. The actual depths vary depending on the type of line used, trolling speed, influence of underwater currents and other factors.

Most divers come in a variety of colors that may help attract walleyes. Precut reflective tape panels also may be purchased for Dipsy Divers.

DIVER TACKLE

"The bigger disk divers pull hard," says Capt. Troxel. "They require rod holders and stout rods."

Several manufactures offer rods specifically designed for diving planes. They generally run from about 7 to more than 10 feet in length and boast strong butt sections with limber tips. Troxel has settled on an 8 1/2-foot model made by Daiwa.

"You need that soft tip," he says, "so you can see the rod rattle when a fish hits. A small fish may not snap the release. If you don't see the strike, you may drag it for quite a while. You have to watch your rods closely and check them regularly."

Light, big-water trolling reels with low gear ratios ease the task of dredging up diving planes. Fill reels with line that withstands the relentless drag of a diving plane. Troxel started out with 20-pound monofilament. Though it served well, he switched to one of the new super-strong braided lines, as have many other anglers who dote on diving planes.

A 25-pound super braid has the diameter of 6- to 8-pound monofilament, so it lets divers run deeper. Because this type of line has virtually no stretch, rods respond more vigorously to strikes, and the releases on the divers break more cleanly. Avoid Dacron braided lines, however, since they prevent divers from reaching maximum depths.

These days, Troxel runs Berkley FireLine. It handles more like monofilament, but retains the virtues of the super braids. However, he still runs a clear, 20-pound monofilament leader to his lure, which he believes is less visible to walleyes.

Capt. Bob Troxel with a big Lake Erie walleye taken on a diving plane and a spoon.

Diving planes require stout rods.

larger No. 1 Dipsy would plow bottom if set that far back in the 40-foot and shallower water that Troxel normally fishes.

In the central and eastern basins, where walleyes regularly swim 55 feet or deeper, the largest directional divers rule. Capt. Andy Emrisko, who docks his 27-foot Wave Walker at Cleveland's Lakefront State Park, usually sets out six No. 1 Dipsy Divers.

To help separate the divers, Emrisko employs three braces of rods in different lengths that rest in three pairs of holders. The two holders on each corner of the transom support 8-foot rods matched with divers set on a 0 or 1 setting. The next pair of holders on the gunnels receive 9-foot rods with Dipsy Divers adjusted to a 2 or 2 1/2 setting. A little farther up the gunnels, a third pair of holders carry 10-foot rods connected to divers adjusted to a 3 or 3 1/2 setting. Each rod reaches farther out than the next, and each Dipsy swims farther out to the side than the next.

"The more line you let out," says Emrisko, "the deeper a Dipsy goes. But once you get much past 150 feet, you hit a neutral point where it goes no deeper.

"Even so, I may run it back 200 feet to get my lure farther away from my boat noise."

When trolling a diver on 200 feet of monofilament, it is extremely difficult to pop the

"A heavy leader doesn't seem to effect the bite," he says, "and I've never snapped a fish off with one."

Many anglers use snubbers when trolling diving planes. Typically a 6-inch length of rubber tubing, a snubber acts as shock absorber between the rod line and the diver. It prevents a sudden jolt, such as bumping bottom or a hard strike from a big fish, from breaking off the diver or the lure. Snubbers are especially important when using lighter leaders.

BASIC SETUPS

Since he trolls primarily in the shallower western basin, Troxel doesn't have to get his divers as deep as anglers do in the central and eastern basins. He relies on his Bottom Line LCG to determine how deep the walleyes are holding and then runs his divers at that depth or slightly above it.

His two outside rods drag No. 1 Dipsy Divers, on a 3 setting, which pulls them well away from the boat. He lets out only enough line to reach the fish he sees suspended on his LCG. The two center rods pull No. 0 Dipsy Divers, the second largest size. He sets them back about 200 feet to intercept fish that may have been bothered by his boat passing overhead. The

Line counter reels work well with diver rods.

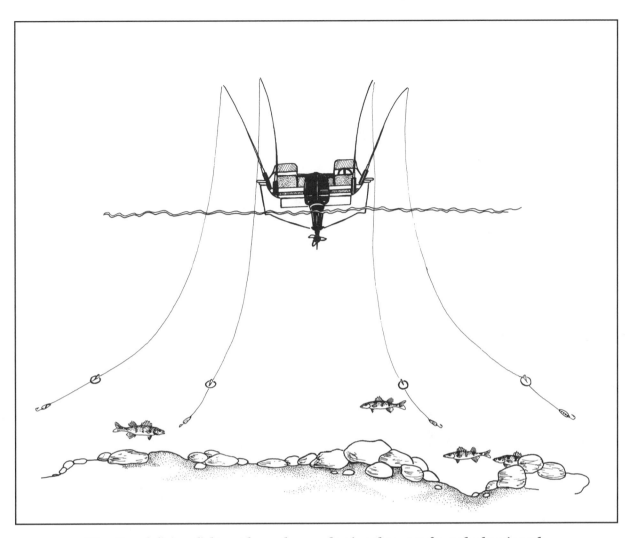

Directional diving disks get lures deep and swing them out from the boat's path.

Capt. Emrisko trolls up to six divers at a time. He uses rods of three different sizes to keep the lines spread. A brace of 8-foot rods on the transom is flanked by 9-foot rods and then a pair of 10-footers.

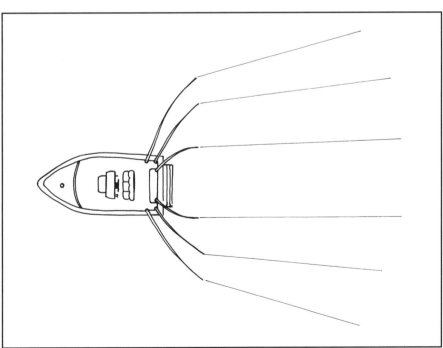

release by sweeping the rod back. Monofilament has too much stretch. This chore must be done many times a day to change or check lures. Here is another instance where a new super line has a clear advantage. Its low stretch lets you free a diver's release with the rod, even on a long line.

When starting out in the morning, Emrisko sets his lines back at different lengths on each side of the boat. The port lines, beginning with the transom rod, may run back 85, 135 and 175 feet. The starboard lines may run 75, 125 and 150 feet. If walleyes show a preference for a particular setup, he duplicates it with the matching rod on the opposite side of the boat.

LURES

Throughout Lake Erie, directional divers sack more walleyes with spoons than any other lure. Spoons grow increasingly effective as the water warms in mid-summer, and they continue producing into the fall. Combine active walleyes with flashing spoons and you've got the makings for a heavy catch.

Clockwise from top left: Northern King 28; Northern King C5S1; Bay De Noc's Flutter Laker Taker; Storm's ThunderStick Jr.; ThunderStick; Thin Fin; Luhr Jensen's Flutter spoon; Pro King.

In the western basin, Troxel dotes on Flash Back Spoons in gold with chartreuse prism tape, and black with green prism tape and a white belly. Other proven colors include silver and white, each dressed with various colors of prism tape. Troxel also favors Bay De Noc's Flutter Laker Taker. Both spoons measure about 4 inches in length.

"Sometimes big spoons put walleyes off," says Troxel. "Dropping down to something like a 2-inch Flute Spoon from Bay De Noc may be what it takes to get them started."

Every spare compartment in Emrisko's cruiser overflows with flat, utility style boxes crammed with lures, most of which are spoons. He owns spoons in every size, color and configuration imaginable. And, of course, he has several of each type, just in case that's what they're hitting on at any given time. It's a wonder his boat stays afloat with all that metal.

A 3 3/8-inch Pentwater Spoon in the 501 pattern has been especially productive for Emrisko. It's pink on one side and black on the other with purple ladderback tape. He also highly recommends the watermelon pattern on any type of spoon. Other spoons that regularly swim behind Emrisko's divers include those made by Pro Spoons, Silver Streak and Northern King. He prefers treble hooks to single hooks and bends the points slightly off center with pliers, which he believes improves their efficiency.

If walleyes ignore standard spoons, Emrisko digs out boxes filled with reflective tape and marking pens in myriad colors to modify existing patterns.

"Change is the name of the game," says Emrisko. "If I have something that's working, I leave it in the water. But if I haven't caught anything for awhile, I change it. Lake Erie's changing. The water clarity's changing. Everything is changing. You've got to change your baits too."

Changes were unnecessary during a hazy July morning aboard the Wave Walker when I joined Emrisko, George McKenzie, Mike Shott, Art Regnelli and Bob Daniel, all northeast Ohio fishermen.

After boating 13 miles north of Cleveland, Emrisko set out four diver rods rigged with spoons. He began putting out boards that would carry additional lines, but was interrupted when a 6-pound walleye slammed a spoon on one of the divers.

After netting the fish, Emrisko went back to work on the boards, but had to stop again to net another fish. He normally sets out board lines in less than 15 minutes. That morning it took him an hour. The walleyes wouldn't leave the spoons alone. By the time the boards were finally set, 10 respectable fish graced our cooler.

Things slowed somewhat after that, with the board rods and the diver rods both taking additional fish. When the sun burned off the haze and the breeze died early in the afternoon, the action slowed considerably.

"It's always tough when the lake gets flat," said Emrisko.

He responded by changing spoons in earnest. When he finally found a pattern that worked—a silver spoon dressed with green ladderback tape—he switched several other rods over to the same combination and managed to fill our limits.

Though spoons account for most of Emrisko's walleyes on divers, he has success with other lures. Capt. Ron Johnson, who makes a habit of winning major walleye tournaments out of Fairport Harbor with diving planes, has added crawler harnesses to the lures he carries aboard his boat, "Thumper."

"The water clarity is unreal," he says. "My techniques have changed. You want to attract the fish, but if you put out too much flash you'll spook them."

Johnson reduces flash when running crawler harnesses by cutting back to one blade. Some of his harnesses sport two treble hooks, which he rigs with three crawlers so they all hang straight. It's a virtual smorgasbord for walleyes.

"When I run spinners," he says, "I troll at about 1.4 to 1.5 miles per hour.

"The problem with crawler harnesses is that they attract a lot of attention from sheephead and other undesirable fish. They pick the bait off your lures, and you may be dragging a small fish without knowing it. That wastes a lot of time."

When walleyes grow aggressive enough to nail spoons, Johnson feeds them hardware. He trolls at a faster clip with spoons, usually from about 2 to 2.4 m.p.h. Emrisko prefers an even faster pace with spoons, from 2.5 to 2.9 m.p.h. He feels that covering more territory pays off better than a slower trolling speed.

Water temperature helps Capt. Pete Alex determine when to get serious with divers. He heads out on Lake Erie's central basin in his Vision Quest charter boat from Erie Angler Marina in Erie, Pennsylvania.

"You don't have to see them on your graph to catch them," says Alex. "When the water temperature gets up around 70 degrees, some walleyes drop down to the 35- to 40-foot range. That's when I start catching more fish with divers."

Shallow running minnow imitators perform well with divers for Alex. He especially likes Storm's ThunderStick, Jr., ThunderStick, and Rattlin' Thin Fin. Early in the morning and on dark days, he goes with purple or green patterns. Firetiger is a proven producer. On sunny days he runs metallic colored lures behind his divers, such as metallic rainbow trout, black/silver and blue/silver.

In the eastern basin, Ted Malota, also acclaimed for his skill with diving planes, runs a variety of lures. This Hamburg, New York, resident frequently teams up with Capt. Bill King who runs his Searcher One out of Chadwick Bay Marina in Dunkirk Harbor, New York. The water clarity in the deep eastern basin exceeds that found anywhere else in Lake Erie, which presents special challenges.

"We've used Dipsy Divers over the past 8 years," says Malota. "We've gotten into finer stuff because of the water clarity caused by the zebra mussels."

One adjustment includes moving up to 10 1/2-foot diver rods that accommodate longer 10-foot leaders made from 10-pound Trilene XT. Malota believes longer, thinner leaders coax strikes from

Another walleye falls for a spoon trailing a diving plane.

walleyes that may shy from divers sporting shorter leaders. He is also convinced that longer leaders allow the spoons to work with a more alluring action when the boat snakes back and forth in "S" turns.

"If you're making "S" turns," says Malota, "the outside diver runs faster. The inside one slows. They're rising and falling like pistons. That's where the majority of our strikes come from."

Lately, worm harness have been working well for Malota and King, particularly a little number flaunting a pink and white willow leaf blade with a silver back ahead of a string of red and white beads.

In midsummer, when the smelt run small, the big hitter for Malota and King is a 2-inch C5 Northern King spoon in black and pink with a silver back. Copper with orange is also good. Later in the season, larger spoons get the call, such as Northern King's 28, and Luhr Jensen's Flutter Spoon in silver and blue.

"We tip all our spoons," says Malota, "with a piece of a crawler just over an inch long. We hook it right through the head so it doesn't effect the spoon's action."

GETTING DEEPER WITH DIVING PLANES

Walleyes in the central and eastern basins often drop below the normal running depths of most diving disks. One way to get divers deeper is by adding weight. With a Dipsy Diver, attach a bead chain sinker between the release and the rod line.

Kastaway's Diver features an eye on its integral bottom weight where you may fasten an additional weight with a snap swivel. The manufacturer, Kulis, Inc., claims that each ounce of extra weight increases the diving depth by about 5 feet.

Wire line affords another option, though it does groove rod guides. Malota claims that his Dipsy Divers have hit bottom 65 feet deep when trolled with wire. The wire line guru in the central basin, Art Lyon of Conneaut, Ohio, relies on 20-pound, single strand Williams or American brand wire for trolling divers.

"They go deeper with wire," says Lyon, "and you get real snappy releases. The rods are a lot more sensitive, too. Wire weakens if you get a kink in it, but guys who use it regularly don't have too much trouble."

OTHER DIVING PLANES

While directional disks comprise the most versatile diving planes, non-directional divers afford other options. Luhr Jensen's Jet Diver, which floats at rest, rates high with Lake Erie anglers. It's available in five sizes that dive from 10 to 50 feet deep in 10-foot increments.

The smaller Jet Divers see the most play on Lake Erie when used in conjunction with trolling boards. See Chapter 11 for more details on this technique.

Luhr Jensen's Deep Six features a trip action release and comes in three sizes that dive to 40, 60 and 90 feet respectively. The company's Pink Lady, billed as the original diving sinker, has a slid bar that eliminates the diving angle when a fish strikes.

The Fish Seeker, from Fish Seeker, dives to depths of 70 feet. When a walleye strikes, it flips over and surfaces.

Only two non-direction divers should be run at any given time, and they should be trolled from opposite corners of the transom to avoid tangling.

Chapter 10

Small Boards

BEFORE THE ZEBRA mussel invasion, boats could often troll right over walleyes in the murky western basin and not spook them. Now that countless mussels filter the water and drastically increase its clarity, walleyes are proving less tolerant and more elusive.

Clear water has long challenged anglers in Lake Erie's central and eastern basins, and the problem grows more acute as the zebra's bring about increasingly transparent conditions. Fishing deeper isn't always the solution, because walleyes commonly suspend less than 35 feet deep, even when the bottom plunges to 80 feet or more.

Walleyes that suspend near the surface in clear water tend to scoot away from a boat passing overhead and escape the lures trailing behind it. Your depthfinder may mark few fish, yet there could be scads of them swimming out of your path. One of the most effective methods for getting a lure out to boat-shy walleyes consists of trolling with small planer boards that connect directly to your lines.

In-line boards typically measure less than 10 inches in length. Their small profile doesn't intimidate walleyes, and their beveled noses propel them—and the lines and lures they carry—away from the boat.

SMALL BOARD BASICS

Setting out a small planer board presents a simple chore. With the boat moving ahead at trolling speed, let a lure out behind the boat as far as you deem necessary.

Capt. Al Lesh hooks a planer board to his fishing line.

Next, engage the reel, grasp the line above the rod tip and place the rod in a holder. Connect the board to the line using whatever attachments come with the unit, usually two pinch-type line releases, or a line release followed by a wire guide. Be aware that some boards come designated for the right or left side of the boat, and they are not interchangeable.

After attaching the board, pull the rod from the holder, drop the board into the water and feed line as it swims out a distance of roughly 50 to 100 feet. The board's bright color, typically yellow or orange, makes it easier to spot.

Then, engage the reel and place the rod back into its holder. The rod should rest in an upright position. This helps hold the line to the board out of the water and improves strike detection. Keep an eye on the board and the rod tip to determine when a walleye has taken the bait. The key indicator is when the board slides backward.

REFINED SMALL BOARD TACTICS

As with any fishing technique, skill and knowledge determine the level of success with small boards. Trolling them randomly produces inconsistent catches. Refined presentations, such as those used by noted professional walleye angler Gary Parsons of Chilton, Wisconsin, are deadly.

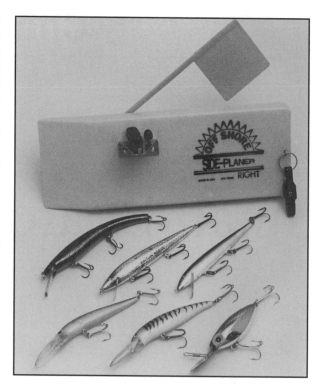

Clockwise from top: Off Shore Side-Planer; Rapala; Hot 'N Tot; Bomber 24A; Deep Jr. ThunderStick; Ripstick; Rattlin Rogue.

Walleye anglers nationwide concede that Parsons is *the* master when it comes to small boards. He has elevated the technique to almost an art form, and deserves much of the credit—along with his close friend Keith Kavajecz—for introducing this tactic to Lake Erie.

"What Keith and I did on Lake Erie," says Parsons, "was help popularize slow-down trolling techniques for post-spawn, deep-water females. Lake Erie had never been exposed to that approach before."

Over the past several years, Parsons and Kavajecz have fished many walleye tournaments on Lake Erie. They have aptly demonstrated that slow trolling with small boards produces excellent catches in the western and central basins, spring through fall. Their methods should work equally well in the eastern basin.

THE PLANER BOARD

In-line planer boards have been around for quite some time, but many of them don't work well with the slow-trolling methods intended for walleyes. Parsons has designed popular boards for several manufacturers and knows which features bring about a superior performance.

"I've been part of the evolution of walleye boards," claims Parsons. "When I mention small

Gary Parsons puts out a small board.

Small boards produce big walleyes from Lake Erie for Gary Parsons.

boards, most people automatically think of the ones designed for salmon trolling at high speeds. They don't work worth a darn for walleyes.

"We troll so slowly that our boards need to be ballasted so they stay upright. Salmon boards, which are not ballasted, tend to fall over at low speeds."

These days, Parsons tows the ballasted (bottom weighted) Off Shore Side-Planer. In addition to its balance, the Off Shore model features two snap-release connectors. They quickly attach and detach from the line and also help the board track true.

When fishing with a partner, Parsons frequently pulls four boards. He says he can take the motor out of gear to land a big walleye, and the remaining three boards hold their positions and stay upright.

A lure stalls when a small board climbs a wave and darts ahead when the board slides down.

"There's no flipping over and no tangling of lines. They just track right out there as you drift," he says.

LURE SPEED

In April, Parsons scores well on heavy, post-spawn walleyes in the western basin trolling at a sluggish .8 to 1.2 m.p.h. A 9.9 to 15 h.p. auxiliary outboard on the transom of his Tracker walleye boat lets him maneuver at crawl speeds.

Considering that walleyes tend to be lethargic in the cold water of early spring, the slow pace seems appropriate. As the water warms above 50 degrees, most Lake Erie anglers increase their trolling speeds. Not Parsons. He stubbornly sticks to his inchmeal pace, even when the water climbs to 70 degrees.

The only time Parsons trolls faster is when Erie's walleye get on a strong spoon bite during the heat of the summer and on into the fall. Spoons require a faster speed to achieve an effective action.

"Day in and day out," says Parsons, "the most effective troll is a slow troll. I firmly believe that the majority of the time—other than in the heat of the summer—the fish are triggered much more by a change of speed than they are buy speed alone."

LURE ACTION

Envision a crankbait swimming steadily through Lake Erie's crystalline water. Even at a depth of 30 feet, enough sunlight filters down to reflect off the lure's bright sides. At some point, the flashing rhythm grabs a walleye's attention. The heavy fish abruptly whirls about, closes on the lure and then tailgates inches behind it for several seconds. Eventually, the walleye loses interest and turns away.

Now reconstruct the same scenario. But just before the walleye turns away, give the lure a sudden stop-go-action. The erratic movement triggers the walleye's strike reflex and the fish nabs the bait. It is this sudden change in action that Parsons strives to impart when trolling.

"Small boards are the absolute best way to do that," stresses Parsons. "When the board races down a wave and stops, it passes that action directly to your lure. And that speed change is a lot more dramatic when you troll at a slow speed. The tow line on a big ski board absorbs some of the shock, so the action is not near as dramatic as with a small board."

To determine just how much action the fish prefer, Parsons may start out running flat lines along with his board lines. The boards, dancing up and down the waves, generate the most energetic lure response. One or two other rods in holders pull flat lines and provide more subtle actions. The remaining flat line rod lays across the bottom of the boat with about a foot of its tip sticking out. It sustains the most subdued lure motion.

"That gives you three different stop-and-go presentations at the same time," says Parsons. "There are times when the rod on the floor catches all the fish, times when the flat lines in the holders are better, and times when the boards—especially on calm days— just cream everything."

TROLL WITH THE WIND

One rule that Parsons sets in stone is: "Always troll with the wind."

This maneuver simplifies boat control and spurs small boards up and down waves with the liveliest action. A flat, calm day makes for poor trolling, because there are no waves to bring the lures to life.

On blustery days, Parsons may pop his kicker outboard in and out of gear to slow the boat. Under extreme conditions, the wind propels the boat and the motor is used only for steering.

The moment Parsons hooks a good walleye, he marks the spot by entering a waypoint in his GPS. After landing the fish, he may continue trolling in the same direction another 500 yards. If no other strikes ensue, he quickly pulls in all the rods, circles around and upwind of the waypoint, and makes another pass through the same area. He continues making passes until he stops catching fish.

"If there's one big walleye there," he says, "you can usually milk three or four more big ones out of that same area. Some schools are tight. You just can't continue trolling for 2 or 3 miles after you catch a fish before turning around."

TACKLE

Parsons and Kavajecz designed a 7-foot graphite trolling rod—part of the Team Daiwa series—that works well with small boards. The medium-heavy rod withstands the resistance caused by a board, plus its trailing weight and lure, without bowing too deeply.

"I don't know that graphite is extremely important," says Parsons, "but the rod's got to be stiff

In early spring, Capt. Lesh takes big Erie walleyes trolling small boards near shore.

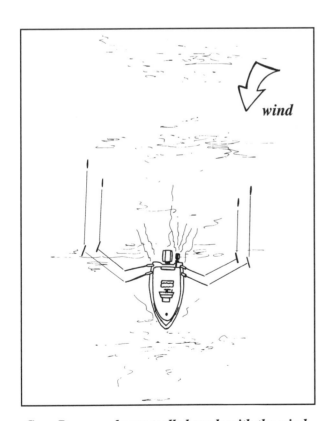

Gary Parsons always trolls boards with the wind.

enough that it doesn't bend over to the point where you can't read it.

"My rods retain a moderate bow, so I don't always have to scan the water and pick out the board. A lot of times, I can glance at my rod tips and know I have a fish on, especially with the big walleyes in Lake Erie. They just double a rod over."

Parsons relies on Daiwa SG27LC line counter trolling reels to put lines out at specific distances and perfectly duplicate productive settings. He fills the spools with 10-pound Trilene XT.

KEY SETUPS FOR SMALL BOARDS

During a two-week period in late March and early April, Capt. Al Lesh of Warren, Michigan, has a field day trolling small boards in the western basin. Lesh concentrates on shorelines east and west of the Maumee River and loads up on big, post-spawn females in shallow water.

"I troll only about 50 yards offshore," says Lesh. "I run small planer boards right up near the bank in 5 feet of water. I've seen walleyes up to 14 pounds come out of that skinny water."

Subtle-action minnow lures swim about 100 feet behind Lesh's boards on 10-pound test monofilament. The shallow running Bomber 15A and No. 13 Rapala,

*Small boards and subtle long minnow lures
are deadly in the spring on Lake Erie.*

Lesh's favorite lures in this situation, wobble freely above the bottom.

The big walleyes soon vacate the shallows and join hordes of other post-spawn females in deeper, western-basin waters. Trolling for these fish with small boards throughout April and into early May presents a prime opportunity for catching limits of heavy fish. At this time, Parsons scours the western basin with his LCG, searching for walleyes out to depths of 40 feet.

"The depth varies so much from year to year," says Parsons, "that you have to let your graph dictate what you should be trying. You find a location that's holding fish and note how deep they are. Sometimes they suspend only 10 feet down.

"You put together potential setups that target the approximate depth zones where you're marking fish. You don't know if any of those fish are walleyes until you catch the first one. If you get a second bite and a third bite, you can start putting together patterns. Tournament fishermen call them programs."

SPRING PROGRAMS

Shallow running minnow lures, such as Storm's ThunderStick, and Jr. ThunderStick, Smithwick's Rattlin' Rogue, and No. 11 and No. 13 floating Rapalas, comprise the basis for Parsons's early spring programs on Lake Erie. He first establishes the most productive trolling depth. After that, he refines lure speed, lure action and lure color.

The old trick of making "S" curves helps determine whether the fish want a faster or slower trolling speed. When a boat turns, the outside boards speed up, while the inside boards slow down. If strikes come consistently from the faster or slower side, Parsons adjusts his speed accordingly.

When Parsons first came to Lake Erie nearly a decade ago, lead core line furnished his primary means for getting minnow lures deep. Today he favors the simplicity and flexibility of Snap Weights. The essentials of lead core trolling and the Snap Weight System are covered in Chapter 8 on basic trolling.

"If it's calm," says Parsons, "I put out nothing but boards. If it's rough, the boat doesn't bother the walleyes as much, so I put out flat lines and boards. In the latter case, the boards mainly spread the lines to cover more water."

Once he settles the boat down to an appropriate tolling speed, Parsons lets out minnow baits with Snap Weights that pull the lures down to the level he wishes to cover. He uses weights from 1/2 ounce to 8 ounces. A small board, however, can only carry a weight up to 3 ounces, which is enough to pull a minnow lure down into the 40- to 50-foot range on a long lead.

After letting the lure back 50 to 100 feet behind the boat—sometimes only 30 feet in murky water—Parsons snaps a weight to the line. He then lets out an additional 20 to 110 feet, depending on the depth he is trying to achieve.

At this point, a rod intended for flat line trolling is placed in a holder. Otherwise, a small board is first attached to the line and allowed to swim out away from the boat. When a walleye nails a lure on a board line, both the board and the snap weight must be removed as the fish is reeled in.

Though Parsons counts on slender minnow lures in the spring, many other anglers also catch walleyes pulling spinner rigs with small boards. As the water warms and walleyes become more active, Parsons makes extensive use of spinner rigs and wobbling crankbaits, such as Rapala's Shad Rap, Storm's diving Jr. ThunderStick and Hot 'N' Tot, and deep diving Bomber Long As.

These lures have performed well for him in both the western and central basins. When starting the day, Parsons commonly trolls a wide variety of lures and lets the walleyes tell him which they prefer.

"I've fished the central basin," he says, "in water out to 80 feet deep. Surprisingly, you get a ther-

When landing a walleye, the board must be removed from the line when it reaches the boat. Here, walleye pro Jim Schiefelbein teams up with Scott Stecher to smoothly perform this task.

mocline that sets up out there anywhere from 35 to 50-some feet deep. The majority of the biting fish are going to be at thermocline level or above, and that's well within the range of small boards."

LANDING WALLEYES

When you notice that a walleye has been hooked, fetch the rod and steadily crank in the board. The boat should continue running at trolling speed. Avoid setting the hook. Doing so may give the walleye enough slack line to escape.

Stop reeling when the board reaches the boat and remove it from the line while maintaining rod pressure on the walleye. Two anglers working in harmony easily perform this task. From this point on, land the walleye as you normally would.

TANDEM BOARDS

When running two boards off the same side of the boat, space them far enough apart to avoid tangles. A good combination is 50 feet out for the inside board and 100 feet out for the outside board. If the boards tow lures that run at different depths, match the shallower running lure to the outside board.

After hooking a walleye on an outside board, the inside board must be adjusted to prevent the lines from tangling while reeling in the fish. This requires teamwork.

One angler holds the outside rod that has the walleye, while another angler quickly feeds line to the inside board. When the inside board drops back well behind the outside board, bring the walleye inside and under the line connected to the outside board.

Another option consists of winding up the inside board and placing it on the opposite side of the boat until the walleye is landed on the outside board.

Chapter 11

Big Boards

Rick LaCourse has experienced the evolution of Lake Erie's fishing methods first hand. A veteran western basin charter captain and an accomplished professional walleye tournament angler, he helped popularize drift fishing with weight-forward spinners nearly 20 years ago.

Possessed by an intense drive to improve his skills, LaCourse has since mastered every prominent fishing technique that has been introduced to Lake Erie. He is adept with jigs, bottom bouncers, spinner rigs and all manner of trolling systems.

When asked how he prefers to catch Lake Erie walleye today, LaCourse answers without hesitation: "Big boards."

Big boards, also known as skis, prevail in the central and eastern basins. LaCourse believes they produce equally well in the western basin because they offer undeniable advantages.

BIG BOARD BASICS

The nose of a board is cut at an angle that makes it swim out away from the boat. Unlike a small board, which tows a single lure, a brace of big boards carry from three to six fishing lines on each side of the boat.

Big boards connect to heavy tow lines, typically 200-pound test Dacron. The lines run through pulleys attached to the hard tops of cruisers or to tall bow masts specifically designed for towing big boards. Mechanical or electric reels store the tow lines.

"The obvious advantage with boards," says LaCourse, "is that I get my lines out away from the boat. My lures are out there doing their thing anywhere from 50 to 200 feet behind the boards. Any walleyes that spook away from my boat run into my board lines."

Big boards tow several fishing lines out away from the boat.

*Tow lines for boards are often
run from masts with large reels.*

*Clockwise from top left: Wally Diver;
Wiggle Wart; Power Dive Minnow; Deep
Ripstick; Bomber 9A; Bomber 25A.*

"And considering that each board is out on 150 feet of tow line, I've got eight to 10 baits covering a swath 200 to 250 feet wide, accounting for the drift-back of the boards."

BIG BOARD ANATOMY

On Lake Erie, boards featuring double and triple skis prevail, such as the triple Super Ski, from Prince Master Craft, that LaCourse favors. A single board handles a few lines, but larger, heavier, multi-ski boards swim farther out, carry heavier loads and maintain better stability in rough seas.

Many anglers make their own boards, including Capt. Andy Emrisko, who docks at Cleveland's Lakefront State Park. Constructed from 1 1/4-inch thick redwood, Emrisko's tandem skis measure 32 x 8 inches. To increase their stability, he drilled a 1/2-

MONOFILAMENT TOW LINES

While braided Dacron is the most popular material for tow lines, some anglers prefer monofilament which is smoother and allows releases to slide more freely. Capt. Lee prefers 220-pound test Ande line. Capt. Johnson buys spools of monofilament used in grass trimmers. He claims it's inexpensive and performs well.

inch hole 6 inches deep into the front and rear of each board just above the bottom edge. Each hole is stuffed with .50 caliber muzzleloader balls.

"Water pressure against a planer board," says Emrisko, "is what pushes it away from the boat. My boards sink better than half way down, so they really get a good grip."

To help keep the tow line out of the water, Emrisko bends up the connecting eye on the board. A 2-foot bungie attaches the eye to the tow line.

"In rough water," says Emrisko, "that bungie takes up the shock and keeps the line good and taut. You still get a little slap in the line, which speeds the lures up and slows them down. Walleyes like that."

BIG BOARD VERSATILITY

Big boards effectively troll just about any lure and line combination normally used for Lake Erie walleye. That includes deep diving crankbaits and a wide variety of lures matched with weighted lines, wire line and small to medium size diving planes.

"The walleyes dictate what I'm going to run off my boards," says LaCourse. "Say I'm out in April after post-spawn females and I'm marking fish tight to the bottom, 35 feet deep. I'll start out trolling crankbaits with Snap Weights to get right down amongst them.

"If I see fish coming up to the 25- to 20-foot range as the day goes along, I'll remove the Snap Weights and run my baits up to the fish. The higher the walleyes, the more aggressive they are. Don't hesitate. Wherever you see the fish, go after them."

LaCourse generally goes after them with a variety of Bomber crankbaits, including the 24A and 25A, which are deep diving, long minnows, plus the Wally Bomber, which is similar to a deep diving, bass-style crankbait. These lures have a reputation for

*Walleye pro Rick LaCourse, a veteran Lake Erie charter
captain, favors big boards for walleyes throughout Lake Erie.*

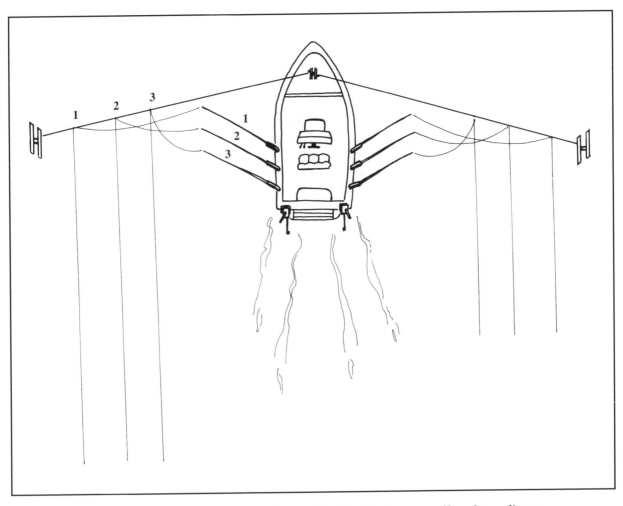

Capt. Andy Emrisko recommends running identical setups off each tow line to avoid confusion and tangles. The rods nearest the bow must have their lines set closest to the boards. The remaining lines must be set in the order shown.

tracking true and are less likely to cause line problems.

"My number one color for Lake Erie is rainbow," says LaCourse, "followed by blue prism flash, firetiger and Tennessee shad, in that order."

Avoid trolling with what LaCourse refers to as "hunting lures," which tend to search erratically to the left and right. While hunting lures do encourage strikes from walleyes, they increase the chances for crossed lines when trolled behind big boards. Jamming lines together on a tow line also invites mishaps.

"I like to keep my baits about 25 feet apart," says LaCourse. "Before you let the line out, swim the bait next to the boat and make sure it's running perfectly true. If it isn't, tune it or replace it."

LaCourse further reduces snarls by putting all the lures connected to a given board back the same distance from the tow line. He may pull a Bomber 25A, 24A and Wally Bomber from the same tow line, but each lure will be, say, 100 feet back. If he adds a Snap Weight to one line, he places the same size Snap Weight the same distance ahead of the other lures. Regardless of which lure a walleye strikes, the hot line clears the others.

"Those three lures," Says LaCourse, "dive within about 5 feet of each other, so they work well together. But if you run the lines back different distances, they don't clear each other when you hook a walleye, and you can't remember how far back each lure has been set."

Trying to keep track of multiple line settings inspires confusion, because the lines continually rotate as walleyes pop them off.

Say, for example, that you hook a fish on the farthest line out on the tow line. After landing the fish, the standard procedure is to let the next line up the tow line slide down and take the place of the one just reeled in. The third line rotates to the second position and so on. The line that hauled in the walleye is reset and takes its place on the tow line nearest the boat.

93

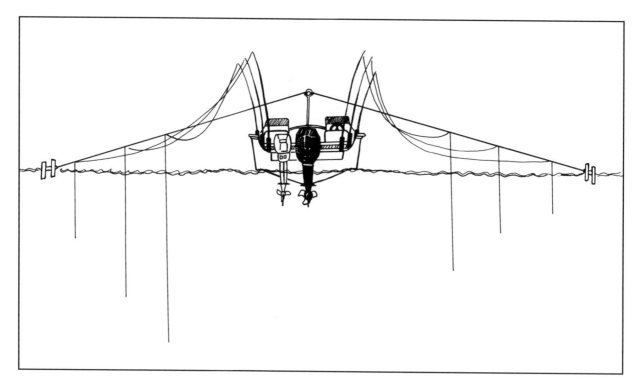

If you choose to stagger the depths, place the shallowest setups out near the boards and the deepest setups close to the boat.

"I don't care what kind of a mind you have," says Emrisko, "sooner or later, you're going to forget what line is where."

Emrisko keeps things simple. He always runs identical setups off a given board, but rarely does he run the same program off both boards.

Ted Malota, an exceptional eastern basin troller from Hamburg, New York, goes against the grain by staggering his board lines. He sets the lines farthest from the boat the shallowest, figuring that they are more likely to intercept walleyes that have not been spooked deeper by the boat. Each line thereafter runs progressively deeper in a descending V, so that the lines closest to the boat swim deepest.

This arrangement avoids tangles, because the shallower outside lines always clear the deeper inside lines. If a walleye comes on the outside line, Malota maintains the V system by popping all the lines free on that tow line and resetting them.

"Its just like an assembly line," he says, "until we find the most productive depth. Then we set 60 to 70 percent of the lines at that depth. We still maintain a few deeper lines, however, because your bigger fish, those 7- to 9-pounders are usually deeper."

DEPTH RANGE FOR BIG BOARDS

Big board trolling regularly plucks walleyes from depths ranging from 15 to 40 feet, even deeper with wire line. I witnessed the shallow end of the spectrum aboard the Sea Screw III with Capt. Jerry Lee of Livonia, Michigan. Lee has been trolling with big boards for nearly 20 years.

We set out at 8 a.m. on a crisp, early July morning with Michigan anglers Tom Wendt, Gary Dickson, Perry Roberson and Bill Clark. Heading out into Michigan's Brest Bay, Lee didn't venture far.

"A recent northeaster brought in dirty water," explained Lee, "so the fish are in shallow."

That morning Lee trolled in water no deeper than 22 feet and as shallow as 12 feet. The floating aquatic vegetation that often collects in Brest Bay and fouls trolling lines had been pushed into shore by the wind. This eliminated a considerable handicap.

Working efficiently, Lee put out a pair of tandem boards. Each board carried five lines set back 40 to 50 feet, and each line pulled a Storm Wiggle Wart.

"In murky water," said Lee, "suspended wall-eyes often feed only 5 to 8 feet deep. Sometimes I run crankbaits only 15 to 20 feet behind the tow lines and slow the trolling speed to keep the plugs up on top.

"When you stop catching fish deep and think they're gone, you may be fishing under them."

Lee opted for metallic colored Wiggle Warts in the dingy water, gold and silver patterns. Despite the shallow water, he also set out a few spoons on Dipsy Divers and downriggers. While the spoons did account for an occasional walleye, the Wiggle Warts behind the boards did the heavy damage.

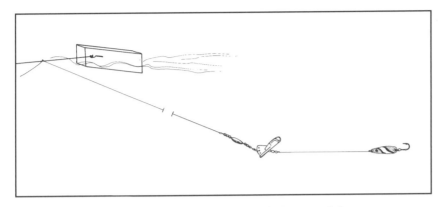

Pulling diving planes behind big boards is one of the most consistent walleye producers in Lake Erie's vast, deep basins.

weights are another effective option for getting lures deeper. They come into play for Capt. Pete Alex, of Erie, Pennsylvania, when the water in the central basin climbs to 70 degrees.

"I put 2- to 3-ounce keel sinkers," he says, "about 3 feet ahead of deep diving ThunderSticks to get them down 35 to 40 feet."

DIVING PLANES

In the central and eastern basins, towing diving planes behind big boards has proven to be an exceptional walleye producer. This combination has paid off royally for Capt. Ron Johnson, who has won big money fishing major walleye tournaments out of Ohio's Fairport Harbor.

Luhr Jensen's Jet Diver, a floating diver, is the primary model for Johnson and many other successful Lake Erie trollers. The Jet Diver comes in five

Walleyes started slamming the Wiggle Warts even before Lee had set out all the lines. After netting a fish, he quickly got the lure back in action. Proficient trollers never stop to admire a fish until all the lines are in the water. Walleyes weighing up to 4 pounds assaulted the crankbaits like clockwork as Lee trolled in a large circle, following a plot line on his GPS. Lee netted doubles twice, and claimed he had to net five fish at once a week earlier.

"A good day," said Lee, "is when you never get all the rods set."

By 10 a.m., a boat limit of walleyes stuffed the cooler and we headed in. It had all happened too quickly.

We've mentioned how LaCourse runs crankbaits deeper with Snap Weights, a tactic that works throughout Lake Erie. Bear in mind that spinner rigs and other lures also perform well with weighted lines. Keel

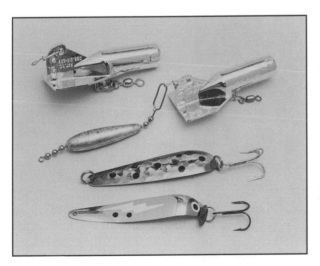

Clockwise from top: No. 20 Jet Diver; No. 10 Jet Diver with bead sinker; Northern King 28; Bay De Noc's Flutter Lake Taker.

Capt. Ron Johnson runs a wide variety of lures behind diving planes pulled by big boards.

sizes—10, 20, 30, 40 and 50—designed to dive to depths ranging from 10 to 50 feet. Johnson uses a variety of sizes and often gets them deeper by attaching 1/2- to 1 1/2-ounce pencil weights between the rod lines and the noses of the divers. Spoons see a lot of action behind Johnson's divers, but he sometimes goes with spinner rigs or crankbaits.

Spoons also get most of the work when Emrisko hitches No. 10 Jet Divers to his boards. He prefers this smallest size because it generates the least resistance when winding it in. Depth variation is achieved by attaching 2- to 4-ounce bead sinkers to the divers.

"For every ounce of weight that you put on a No. 10 Jet Diver," says Emrisko, "you're going to gain 3 to 5 feet of depth. So with 4 ounces, you're looking at about 30 feet."

Three Jet Divers on each board line comprise Emrisko's basic spread. He simplifies things by running a different program on each board. All the spoons on the port side, for example, could be 150 feet back on No. 10 Jet Divers with 2 ounces of weight; while all the starboard spoons may be back the same distance on No. 10 Jet Divers with 4 ounces of weight. If one board produces more strikes, Emrisko switches the other board to the same program.

As do many other charter captains, Emrisko sets out large diving disks and downriggers inside the board lines to reach deeper fish. On a typical outing, boards, diving disks and downriggers all produce fish. Trolling a wide depth range insures that you don't bypass a school of walleyes without presenting a lure to them.

WIRE LINE

For the deepest presentations with big boards, Art Lyon of Conneaut, Ohio, trolls with Williams or American brand 10- or 12-pound test single strand wire line. With 300 feet of wire out, a Bomber 25A digs below 60 feet. When I fished the central basin several years ago with Lyon, his brothers Bruce and Russ, plus some of their offspring, they ran as many as six lines off each board.

The heavy resistance of that many deep diving plugs on wire line is too much for most commercially made boards, so Lyon constructs what could be called magnum tandem planer boards. Each board is comprised of two 48 x 8 x 1 1/4-inch slabs of redwood which are held together with Plexiglas or aluminum brackets.

Today, Lyon puts out smaller boards that each troll three crankbaits on wire lines at moderate depths. For the deepest presentations, he now runs disk divers on wire line.

SPEED WITH BIG BOARDS

As with other trolling methods, the trolling speed depends on the season, water temperature, water clarity, mood of the fish and the lures being trolled. In cold water and when trolling spinner rigs anytime, hold speeds under 1.5 miles per hour. In warmer water, and especially with spoons, most charter captains recommend a faster pace, say, 1.5 to 3 miles per hour. Dingy water generally dictates a slower trolling speed even in warm water.

TACKLE

A 7- to 9-foot medium action trolling rod with a matching reel and 10-pound line serves well with big boards. Sensitive graphite rods aren't necessary, because you see the strikes by watching the rod tips and the releases.

LaCourse opts for 7-foot medium action St. Croix trolling rods paired with SpiderWire's 12-pound Fusion line. Fusion looks and handles more like monofilament, yet retains the thin diameter, superior strength and low stretch capabilities of the super braids.

Lee fills his reels with Mason 35-pound test braided line—a super braid—and runs a monofilament leader to his lures. He is especially fond of

Rick LaCourse sets out sea anchors on each side of the boat to slow his trolling speed.

the medium-light fiberglass trolling rods that he designed for Eagle Claw. He believes that a soft rod combined with a low-stretch braided line affords better hookups and a more distinct feel of the fish during the fight. Emrisko agrees.

"I run 20- or 30-pound Mason braided line on everything except downriggers," he states. "It gives you a better hook set and cleaner releases when a walleye strikes. And you can really feel just how much tension you've got on a fish."

Emrisko runs heavier monofilament leaders off his Jet Divers than most anglers, usually 25- to 30-pound test. He reasons that leaders take a beating and result in more lost fish than any other factor. A heavy leader also better withstands the sudden, jolting strike of a steelhead, which occurs regularly these days in the central and eastern basins.

"A lot of people disagree with me," says Emrisko. "They say thinner leaders catch more fish. Well, I'll compare my box to anybody's at the end of the day."

Jim Stedke super-tunes a crankbait.

that require major surgery. While circling, your boards spend some of their time bucking against the waves and running diagonally across them. This often yields fewer bites, but not necessarily. Sometimes a change in trolling direction increases the action.

"Pay attention to the current and the direction of the troll," advises Jim Stedke of Lima, Ohio, a longtime Lake Erie fisherman with an almost legendary reputation. "Sometimes only one direction produces fish."

THE WIDE ADVANTAGE

In a nutshell, big boards present a wide variety of lures at various depths and greatly extend the width of the trolling pass. They let you cover a bigger chunk of Lake Erie more efficiently than any other method.

"During the course of a charter," says LaCourse, "I may troll at 2 miles per hour for 5 or 6 hours. I've cut a swath 250 feet wide for 12 miles, and my lures are working 100 percent of the time.

"From a mathematical standpoint, no other technique covers as much water or presents my baits to as many walleyes. You can't beat the odds."

WITH THE WIND

As with small boards, trolling downwind with big boards provides better control and makes the boards race and stall, which brings about a more lively lure action. The drawback with big boards is that it takes considerable time and effort to bring in all the lines, plus the boards, and reset them. You can't simply pull in the lines and circle around for another pass over the same area, as may be done when trolling with a few small boards.

Under ideal conditions, you can often troll for great distances with the wind and continue catching walleyes. On most days, however, you must make large circles and swing back over schools of fish. Turning too sharply crosses lines and creates tangles

SUPER-TUNING CRANKBAITS

Never troll a crankbait that doesn't run true, especially when trolling with boards. Jim Stedke always drops a lure over the side and checks it before hooking it to his tow line. With the boat running at trolling speed, Stedke rips the lure forward several times with his rod.

"If the lure immediately digs in and dives," he says, "it's running right. Many lures run all right at a steady speed, but veer to the side when pulled sharply ahead. On a rough day, when the board lines are popping and snapping, your lures are repeatedly being jerked ahead. That's why you have to super-tune them."

*Rick LaCourse sends a
release down a tow line.*

If a crankbait fails to track true when ripped ahead, Stedke gently bends the line eye on the bill with needle nose pliers. Bending the eye to the left makes the lure run to the left and vice versa. Stedke continues checking the lure and adjusting the eye until the bait is super-tuned or fails the test. Not all baits pass muster, even brand new lures.

SETTING LINES

After letting a lure out behind the boat an appropriate distance, snatch the line above the rod tip and place the rod in a holder. Then insert the line into a release that is fixed to a shower curtain ring or a similar device. Snap the shower curtain ring around the tow line.

Next, feed line off the reel as the lure's resistance slides the release down the tow line toward the board. When the release is positioned where you want it, engage the reel and take up enough slack to put a slight bow in the rod tip. Repeat this procedure until all the rods have been set, spacing the releases along the tow line to prevent tangles.

RUBBER BAND RELEASES

These days, many anglers connect their fishing lines to releases with rubber bands. Simply fold the rubber band around the line where you wish to con-

nect a release. Then run one end through the other and pull the rubber band snug. Place the end of the rubber band's loop in the release and set it out as usual.

The rubber band helps prevent premature releases, especially on rough days. Some anglers claim that rubber bands also reveal when a line is towing a fish, since the affected rubber band stretches farther back than the others.

Capt. Andy Emrisko makes his own rubber band releases by soldering small alligator clips to shower curtain rings. The rubber bands can't slip out of the clips, so they must be broken to free the lines. Emrisko feels this is more consistent than conventional releases.

EASY REACH

A standard item when trolling with big boards is a cord that that fastens to the boat's gunnel on one end and to a ring around the tow line on the other. When you wish to attach a release to the tow line, which is generally well out of reach, simply pull the line close with the cord.

POPPING LINES FROM RELEASES

When trolling with big boards, you must snap lines from releases many times each day to check and change lures. Even when walleyes strike, they don't always free lines from the releases, so you must do so.

If you crank up every bit of slack and then pull, the line stubbornly sticks in the release. The proper way to go about it is to take up only part of the slack. Then quickly drop the rod tip and snap it back. This whips the rod upward and efficiently frees the line.

PECKING ORDER FOR RODS

Rods for big boards must be placed in holders fixed along the gunnels in a particular order. The rod with the line farthest out toward the board must be in the holder nearest the bow. The rod with the second line out occupies the holder next to the first rod. Continue this order until the rod with the line closest to the boat rests in the holder nearest the transom.

The above arrangement prevents tangles and confusion, because the farther lines always clear over the nearer lines. The exception is the nearest line, which doesn't have to clear anything. Simply pull the live rod from the holder, hold the tip high until the line passes over the other rod tips and you're in business. You never lose tension on the walleye.

Place the rods in holders in any other order, however, and you must drop some rods beneath other lines and pass them around other rods to clear them. Avoid this route, unless you enjoy chaos.

When trolling with big boards, the rods must be placed in a particular order to prevent tangles. Watching the rod tips reveals strikes.

FELT MARKERS

Jet Divers come in a variety of colors which may very well help attract walleyes. If he doesn't have the color diver he wants, Jim Stedke pulls out an assortment of felt markers and "paints" the hue he desires.

The markers also come in handy for altering spoons, crankbaits and other lures.

TOW LINE EFFECTS LURE DEPTH

Even when running identical lures the same distance back on a tow line, they will not dive to exactly the same depth. That's because the tow line starts out high at the boat and descends to water level at the board.

"If your inside lines are going and your outside lines aren't," says Capt. Ron Johnson, "your far lines are running below the fish. Shorten the leads on the far lines and all your lures will start producing."

Chapter 12

Downriggers

J OE DEBUYSSER of South Bend, Indiana, remembers a walleye tournament he fished some 20 years ago in the western basin. In all his 50 years of fishing Lake Erie, he never got more attention.

"Press photographers," he says, "followed me around all day to take pictures of my downriggers. They'd never seen them used on Lake Erie before. I came in second place using nothing but downriggers."

These days, DeBuysser docks at Foxhaven Marina on Catawba Island and still relies on downriggers. He usually sets out downriggers and directional disk divers, adjusting the divers so they swim out away from the downrigger lines. The downriggers consistently take as many walleyes as the divers.

Though downriggers commonly sprout from boat transoms in the deeper central and western basins, they aren't nearly as popular in the shallower western basin. Many anglers regard them only as tools for running lures deeper than other trolling methods can reach. Truth is, downriggers afford excellent depth control in any water.

A boat sporting downriggers trolls the open expanses of Lake Erie for deep walleyes.

A Lake Erie walleye angler hooks his line to a release before sending the cannonball deep.

DOWNRIGGER ANATOMY

All downriggers feature large plastic or aluminum reels that hold 135- to 150-pound test steel cable. With manual models, you wind the cable with a crank. With electric models, a small motor does the work. The cable connects to a downrigger weight, called the cannonball or bullet, depending on its shape. A footage counter reveals how deep the cannonball is lowered.

A boom arm extends from the reel and holds the cable out over the edge of the boat. The release for the fishing line connects directly to the cannonball or to the cable just above it. You hook your sport line to the release and lower the cannonball to the desired depth. When a walleye strikes, the line snaps out of the release. You then fight the fish freely on light line, such as 10-pound test monofilament.

Special downrigger rods typically measure 6 to 8 feet. They feature limber actions because their lines carry only lures. The rods also must maintain deep bows when set in holders, so they pop straight up after a strike. This helps take up slack line and alerts you that a fish is on. Rod holders usually clamp to the backs of downriggers, but they may be placed in other locations.

Downriggers are not limited to big boats. The wide transoms of large cruisers may support four to six downriggers, but smaller fishing boats easily handle two. Most downriggers attach to deck supports that mount permanently in place. Miniature, portable downriggers, however, are available. These clamp to transoms or gunnels.

DOWNRIGGER APPLICATIONS

In the western basin, DeBuysser's faith in downriggers is the exception. Most anglers who employ downriggers here typically put down one or two cannonballs to compliment their disk divers and boards. That was Capt. Jerry Lee's strategy the day I fished with him and a group of his clients in Brest Bay near Monroe, Michigan.

Big boards towing crankbaits took the bulk of the catch, while a few divers and downrigger lines managed occasional bonus fish. Lee set the cannonballs only 14 feet deep with spoons following 10 to 15 feet behind. It surprised me that walleyes hit the spoons right after the boat rumbled directly over their heads. Did the murky water prevent the boat from alarming the fish?

"I disagree with guys who say walleyes are spooky," says Lee. "Walleyes aren't spooky at all."

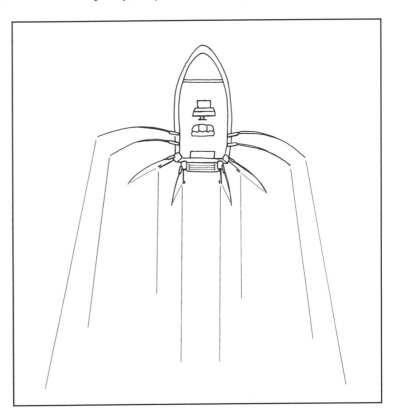

Joe DeBuysser runs downriggers on the transom and diver rods on the gunnels.

DeBuysser echoes Lee's sentiments. He scores as well now with his downriggers in the western basin as he did when the water was dingy.

"I catch a lot of fish in this clear water 14 to 16 feet deep on downriggers," he says. " I don't believe the boat spooks them. If they're feeding, you're going to catch them."

DeBuysser trolls mainly west of Kelleys Island in water 30 to 32 feet deep. He puts his downriggers and divers into play early in April and continues taking fish with them well into the fall.

In early spring, he trolls 2-inch Little Cleo spoons 6 to 10 feet behind cannonballs set 14 to 18 feet deep. This fat little spoon displays an erratic fluttering action at slow trolling speeds.

"When the water is still cold," says DeBuysser, "I slow down to about .9 miles per hour. When the water warms, I troll at 1.5 to 2 miles per hour."

With faster trolling speeds, DeBuysser switches to larger Pro King and Flash Back spoons. The action with suspended, feeding walleyes generally remains steady until the first part of July. From then on, DeBuysser usually sets his downrigger lines deeper.

"They get lazy when the water warms up," says DeBuysser, "and they stay on the bottom. That may be because they're feeding more at night in the clear water. If I'm fishing in 30 to 32 feet of water in the summer, I set my downriggers at 28 to 20 feet. I let the spoons back as much as 30 feet."

DEEPER WITH DOWNRIGGERS

In the central and eastern basins, downriggers present lures to deep walleyes with unsurpassed precision. With other trolling methods, determining the depth requires more guesswork. With downriggers, you know for certain how deep the cannonball is set.

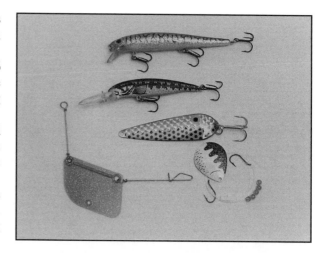

Clockwise from top: Storm ThunderStick; Bomber 24A; Pro King spoon; Quick Change spinner rig; Luhr Jensen trolling rudder.

In the eastern basin, walleyes frequently hold 60 to 80 feet down, and some come more than 100 feet deep! Definitely, this is downrigger territory.

Many experienced anglers believe the biggest walleyes consistently come from deeper water. Capt. Andy Emrisko, who runs charters out of Cleveland, believes trophy walleyes move and feed infrequently and prefer bigger forage. An 11-pound walleye that Emrisko dredged up with a downrigger had a 10-inch perch in its belly.

"I almost filleted the perch," he says.

Fishermen in the crystalline central and eastern basins almost unanimously believe that walleyes shy from boats and cannonballs. They set downrigger lines deep and put lures back as much as 300 feet.

Though spoons are primary lures for downrigger fishing throughout Lake Erie, other offerings produce strikes. This includes the whole gamut of crankbaits. Bear in mind that you must consider a crankbait's additional diving depth. Say, for example, that you want to troll 50 feet deep with a crankbait that dives 6 feet deep. Lower the ball to 44 feet so the lure swims where you want it.

Never forget that walleyes readily move

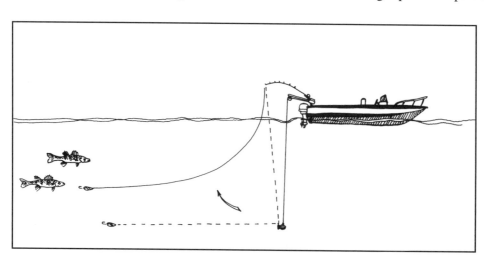

Capt. Bill King triggers strikes by jerking lures from their releases and letting them rise through schools of walleyes.

Precision trolling with downriggers nets walleyes throughout Lake Erie.

up to take lures, but rarely dip down to get them. When you mark fish on a depthfinder, set downrigger lines so your lures swim at the level of the fish or a few feet above them.

Spinner rigs dressed with crawlers take walleyes on downriggers as well. Ted Malota, an eastern basin trolling ace, runs a spinner rig 8 feet behind a plastic trolling rudder that provides stability. He then sets the rudder 200 to 300 feet behind the cannonball.

Malota and Capt. Bill King, of Searcher One Charters in Dunkirk, New York, trigger many strikes by jerking spoons and spinner rigs from their releases. This lets the lures rise and goads strikes from walleyes that may be following them. It also pulls the lures up through fish suspended above the cannonballs.

"I usually watch the graph," says King. "When I see a nice school of fish, we pop a couple of lures free and put the rods back into their holders. Nine times out of 10, the poles bend down with fish on them. That's a real good trick."

REFRAIN FRESHWATER FLEAS

Anyone who trolls Lake Erie in the summer and fall is familiar with the spiny water flea. A non-native aquatic organism, this tiny crustacean collects on downrigger cables and fishing lines and can foul lures. Ted Malota counters this pest by placing a tiny split shot about 30 inches above a lure.

"All the fleas," he says, "catch on the rod side of that split shot. It keeps your swivel from bogging down and affecting the action of lure."

Chapter 13

After Dark

EVOLUTION HAS given walleyes bulging eyes that furnish them with superior night vision. Hidden by darkness, walleyes see their prey better than their prey sees them. This is a critical advantage and walleyes prudently make the most of it.

In Lake Erie's clearer water, walleyes move up to feed at night, often to shallow reefs and close to shorelines. Every year more anglers venture forth after the sun goes down and reward themselves with excellent catches.

Angelo Zito of Seven Hills, Ohio, demonstrated just how good night fishing can be in 1993 when he caught a 15-pound, 13-ounce, walleye while casting from the shoreline near the Marblehead lighthouse on Ohio's Catawba Island. His trophy reigned as the Ohio state record walleye for little more than a year when a 15.95-ounce Lake Erie walleye claimed the title.

Zito's trophy fish inhaled a 3 1/2-inch Countdown Rapala on December 20, but that's only part of the story. Between 8 and 10 p.m. that night, Zito and two of his fishing buddies caught three limits of walleyes. With the exception of the state record, each fish weighed between 7 and 9 pounds.

Many regard the nighttime bite as a new phenomenon. For Capt. Jim Fofrich—one of a small number of walleye captains who now offer night charters—after dark forays bring back pleasant memories of his youth.

"In the early '50s," he says, "I'd go out at night with my dad in a row boat with a small motor. We'd hang a Coleman lantern over the side on a bracket

In Lake Erie's clearer water, walleyes have grown more nocturnal in their feeding habits.

and drift. The light would attract minnows and we'd dip them right out of the lake for bait. We'd fish with spreaders. If you fished right in the light, you'd catch white bass. When you dropped your minnows down below the light or out to the edge of the light, you'd catch walleye and sauger.

"Back then, you'd see 500 lanterns off Port Clinton at night floating on the horizon. You'd look out at the lake from Cleveland and see maybe a thousand lights. It looked like a city. They caught a lot of blue pike at night there."

When Lake Erie's walleye population declined in the '60s and early '70s and blue pike became extinct, Fofrich fished at night only in his memory. As the walleye population rebounded and the lake's water quality steadily improved due to anti-pollution regulations, he resumed his affair with summer nights.

REEFS

Fofrich rekindled his love for night fishing by casting weight-forward spinners, long minnow lures, Rat-L-Traps and diving crankbaits over shallow, western basin reefs. Even reefs that are devoid of walleyes during the day often teem with fish after dark. Two approaches with this method include drifting quietly with the wind or current, or casting from an anchored boat.

"You'll catch fish all over those reefs," says Fofrich. "But if you make too much noise or shine a light on the water, those fish are gone. The party's over."

Though night fishing is effective in the spring, Fofrich holds off until about mid-June. Western basin walleye feed so heavily in the early part of the season that his clients have little trouble catching fish during daylight hours. Once summer commences, however, walleyes become more nocturnal and nighttime outings yield heavier catches.

FLOAT A LANTERN

To prevent his clients from losing too much sleep, Fofrich heads out a few hours before sunset and

Sunset marks the beginning of prime fishing time on Lake Erie.

returns to the dock three to four hours after dark. Before the group begins fishing, he frequently steals a page from his youth and anchors an inner tube that supports a lantern on a wooden platform. He calls this, "setting the dinner table."

Fofrich fishes elsewhere as the waning daylight expires and lets the lantern works its magic. By the time he returns after dark, insects swarm the lantern above the water while throngs of bait fish stream about in the light below the surface. The occasional splash of a feeding fish breaks the silence. At times, the eerie reflection of a walleye's eye flashes back from the perimeter of the light.

"The world shrinks to the size of an inner tube and its light," says Fofrich. "No other fishing affects the Psyche so deeply. It's just you and the fish. Absolute serenity. Beautiful."

A silent electric motor sneaks Fofrich and his party within casting range of the light. Walleyes feeding near the surface pounce on Rat-L-Traps and long minnow lures, such as the Rapala. Walleyes hanging deep may be

---

TIMING

Starting out before daylight or extending an evening trip an hour or two into the night lets you tap the walleye's nocturnal feeding movement without sacrificing a good night's sleep. To get in on the predawn activity and increase the odds for big fish, Capt. Jim Fofrich often leaves the dock with daytime charters at 4 a.m. When fishing after sunset, diligence pays off.

"Right after dark and just before daylight is best," says Fofrich, "but they're likely to hit anytime. You may fish for five hours without a strike and then slam a limit of big ones in five minutes. They may leave just as suddenly as they show up."

*Capt. Jim Fofrich often puts out a lanturn after dark
to attract bait fish and the walleyes that feed on them.*

reached by counting down weight-forward spinners. In some instances, the fish hold 20 feet deep in more than 30 feet of water. Drifting just off the edge of the light while dragging crawler harnesses also takes deep fish.

"One quiet, moonless night," says Fofrich, "I anchored a lantern over 26 feet of water near Niagara Reef. We came back later throwing Rat-L-Traps and caught 75 walleyes."

SHORE FISHING AT NIGHT

Casting from the bank has, by far, become the most popular form of night fishing on Lake Erie, especially since Zito caught his record walleye in 1993. In the western basin, crowds of anglers stand shoulder to shoulder when walleyes move shallow in the fall. The peak fishing typically begins in late October—after most boats have been pulled from the water—and extends until the lake freezes. Bank fishing picks up again in the spring with reports of good catches continuing into June.

The clearer water brought about by zebra mussels may have increased night feeding activity among walleyes, but bank fishing opportunities probably always existed and were overlooked by most anglers. One exception is Capt. Pat Chrysler, who has been shore fishing successfully at night on South Bass Island since he got out of the service in the early '70s.

In October, Chrysler begins seining emerald and spottail shiners from the rocky shorelines of South Bass Island. He later supplies the minnows to his ice fishing clients who fly out to the island during the winter. He caters to as many as 20 ice fishermen a day who go through 50 to 90 gallons of minnows each winter. That's a lot of seining.

Almost every night until ice-up, Chrysler dons waders and seines the shallows under the pale light of a lantern. After making a pass with the seine, which disperses the minnows, Chrysler casts a crankbait for walleyes while the minnows regroup. Night after night, he alternates between a fishing rod and a seine and loads his freezer with walleyes in the process.

In the spring, Chrysler catches walleyes at night from the bank until the first warm weekend brings out a flotilla of boats. The heavy traffic pushes the walleyes deeper and bank fishing abates until autumn.

Casting from the bank at night at Marblehead produces big walleyes.

When word got out that Chrysler and other islanders were taking walleyes at night, a handful of anglers tried the same thing on the mainland and enjoyed instant success. Capt. Dave Demeter was among the first to do so on Catawba Island.

I fished with Demeter once on a crisp, still night in November. He shined a flashlight into the water just out from the riprap bank and revealed why shoreline fishing is so productive during the late season. As far as the beam could reach, the surface was alive with bait fish. It was a virtual walleye smorgasbord.

"Any breakwall or protrusion along the shoreline," said Demeter, "has the potential to attract bait fish and the walleyes that feed on them. All you need is 5 feet of water with a rock or sand bottom. A bright light on the shoreline helps draw them in, but it really isn't necessary."

On November and December nights, anglers crowd Michigan's Luna Pier and the Ohio shorelines of Catawba Island, Huron and Lorain. The action picks up again in the spring, and this is when anglers also take walleyes casting from banks in Pennsylvania. Spring bank fishing opportunities may exist in New York, but the night fishing there is done primarily by anglers in boats.

BANK BAITS

Subtle, shallow-running minnow crankbaits account for the majority of nighttime walleyes. Proven lures include the Rapala and Countdown Rapala, Bomber's 15A, Smithwick's Rattlin' Rogue, Storm's ThunderStick and Reef Runner's Ripstick.

A steady, slow to medium speed retrieve works well, as does a pull-and-pause action. Several minnow baits are available in suspending models that hang in place or rise slowly during long pauses. This trick often triggers strikes. Also try twitching floating minnow lures just beneath the surface. Experiment. On any given night, walleyes frequently show a preference for a particular lure action.

Rattling baits, such as the Rat-L-Trap, Cordell's Super Spot and Rapala's Rattlin' Rap, are also heavy hitters for nighttime walleyes. These lures cast well for distance and coax strikes with everything from slow, bottom-bumping presentations to hot retrieves. They put off tremendous vibrations and high-pitched rattling sounds that spark walleyes into action.

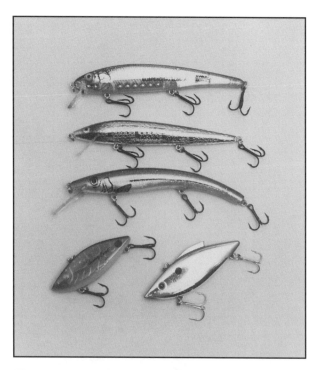

From top: Bomber Suspending Long A; Rattlin' Rogue; Ripstick; Super Spot; Rat-L-Trap.

Whatever the lure, standard bait fish colors score well at night, including silver, gray, gold and chartreuse patterns.

A 6 1/2-foot medium-action spinning or baitcasting outfit does a nice job of serving up minnows and rattling baits after dark. For minnow baits, many anglers prefer spinning tackle which delivers longer casts.

FISH NEAR SHORE FROM A BOAT

A boat lets you fish shorelines and near-shore humps and drop-offs that are off-limits to bank fishermen. Such places abound, and they give up big walleyes to the same lures and methods that work so well when fishing from the bank. This approach produces good catches in the fall and spring in the western basin, and along rocky and gravel shorelines in the central and eastern basins in the spring.

A walleye boat rigged with a small kicker outboard and a bow-mounted electric motor is an ideal setup. You can use the electric motor for sneaking within casting range of shorelines and underwater structures. It also doubles for silently trolling flat lines and in-line planer boards. When you're confronted by a stiff wind, troll with the kicker outboard.

We used a variety of methods when I fished with professional walleye champion Mark Brumbaugh during a mid-October outing near Huron, Ohio. D'Arcy Egan, who covers the outdoor beat for the *Cleveland Plain Dealer,* made us a threesome.

Brumbaugh, a resident of Pittsburgh, Ohio, explained that few walleyes had begun feeding at night tight to the bank, but they were likely to move up on humps in 8 to 10 feet of water.

We idled west from the mouth of the Huron River around midnight. Brumbaugh studied the bright screen of his LCG. It marked plenty of bait fish and occasional long arches that we hoped were walleyes. Stars shone brightly in the blackness overhead. Lights from buildings dotted the mainland, less than a quarter of a mile away. It might as well have been another world.

When Brumbaugh found a ledge 8- to 12-feet deep that dropped into 17 feet of water, he set out four in-line boards, each towing a different long minnow bait. Our first pass along

Walleye pro Mark Brumbaugh sets out a board on Lake Erie after dark.

Mark Brumbaugh takes many big walleyes from Lake Erie at night.

Mark Brumbaugh nets a late night Lake Erie walleye for writer
D'Arcy Egan who covers outdoors for the "Cleveland Plain Dealer."

the ledge—pushed by a small outboard—produced two walleyes, the largest weighing about 7 pounds. Both had come on a smoke Reef Runner Ripstick.

"Do you think we can catch them casting?" said Egan, reading my mind.

"Let's find out," said Brumbaugh.

Brumbaugh returned to the starting point by retracing the boat's trolling path on the plotter of his GPS. He set the boat adrift and maneuvered along the drop-off with the bow electric. We all pitched Ripsticks downwind to avoid having our casts snubbed by a blustery south wind. Brumbaugh soon landed a sizable walleye. Egan boated another minutes later. Then the wind pushed us off the shelf.

"Drag your lines," instructed Brumbaugh, "we'll troll back and make another pass."

He kicked his electric motor on high. We could feel the minnows throbbing our rod tips. When the boat passed over the ledge in 8 to 10 feet of water, our minnows ticked bottom. Suddenly, Egan popped a walleye. Then it was my turn.

On the next casting drift, an 8-pound walleye slammed my lure, the biggest fish of the night. After a few more productive trolling and casting passes, we headed in. Though Brumbaugh's live-well held an impressive mess of fish, it was a mediocre night for

NIGHT LIGHTS

Many bank fishermen bring lanterns, figuring that the light will attract bait fish and, in turn, walleyes. Lanterns also help you see what you're doing and serve as welcome hand-warmers on cold nights.

Regulations require that you keep your running lights on when fishing from a boat at night. Other lights, however, should be kept to a minimum. Keep a flashlight handy, but use it sparingly and avoid shining the beam on the water.

Champion walleye fisherman Mark Brumbaugh fixes a light to the side of his console with suction cups and aims it at the floor. It provides enough illumination for selecting lures, tying knots and performing other chores, yet the light doesn't spill out onto the water.

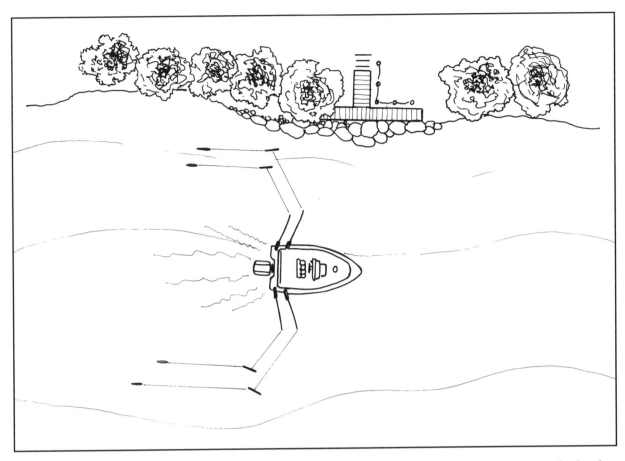

When walleyes feed close to shore at night, Mark Brumbaugh trolls planer boards tight to the bank.

Lake Erie. On several after dark outings, Brumbaugh and a fishing companion have taken double limits of walleyes comprised of fish weighing 10 pounds or more. His largest weighed 12 1/2 pounds.

Brumbaugh does especially well pulling shallow minnow lures 30 to 40 feet behind in-line boards when walleyes move up to banks during fall feeding sprees. He tapes Glow Sticks to the flags of his Off Shore Side-Planer boards so he can see them in the darkness. He trolls parallel to the shoreline just fast enough to make the lures wobble. The outside board runs close to the bank in 3 to 4 feet of water.

"Most fish come on the board running against to the bank," says Brumbaugh, "but sometimes they come on the boards in deeper water.

"The key is finding the bait," says Brumbaugh. "On calm, clear days, I look for banks that hold shad. If I find a place where the bottom turns black with bait fish, I'll come back there at night. When I catch a fish trolling, I swing around and make another pass. If I catch more fish from the same spot, I may anchor and cast to them."

To help walleyes find his lures at night, Brumbaugh anoints them with a short strip of Fish

Formula Glow-Gel which gives off an attracting scent and a fluorescent radiance. After energizing the gel with a flashlight or a camera strobe, it emits an eerie glow for up to 40 minutes.

"As the light diminishes," says Brumbaugh, "it becomes more effective."

In the Michigan portion of the western basin, Capt. Jerry Lee of Livonia, Michigan, reports that walleyes are being taken at night from shallow weed beds. The thin vegetation is just beginning to take hold and grows about 2 feet high out to depths of 8 feet. The weeds contribute fertile hunting grounds for walleyes.

"Just go out there," says Lee, "and crank a Rapala, ThunderStick or any shallow diving minnow bait over the weeds."

Eastern basin walleye wizard Ted Malota from Hamburg, New York, recommends trolling long minnow lures on flat lines along in-shore areas 6 to 10 feet deep. This practice yields good catches of post-spawn walleyes when the season opens there in May.

"Set a Rapala back on 100-125 feet of line," says Malota. "Weight it with a little split shot. The firetiger pattern has been really hot ."

Chapter 14

Winter Locations

WINTER FISHING on Lake Erie begins in January. Yes, bank fishermen in the western basin do cast into open water at night throughout December. But in January, ice in the island area grows thick enough to tread upon. Drilling holes through hard water, jigging spoons and blade baits tipped with minnows—now you're talking *real* winter fishing.

Although ice develops in other regions of Lake Erie, only a portion of the western basin sustains reasonably safe ice, and that ice forms over multitudes of walleyes. By January millions of walleyes have returned to the island area in preparation for their spring spawning movements. The fishing peaks during the latter part of the season, which may extend into March depending on weather.

The No. 1 priority for a successful ice fishing trip on Lake Erie is safety. Never venture on to questionable ice. If you're unsure about where and how to go about it, consider hiring an ice fishing charter, at least for your initial outing.

"You can't trust ice on the open lake," says Capt. Pat Chrysler, who has been a prominent ice guide on South Bass Island for three decades. "There's nothing to hold it in place. You may see ice along the bank somewhere, and then you get an offshore wind that blows it away."

FIRST ICE

"Some of the safest and earliest ice," says Chrysler, "forms west of the Bass islands where I fish. The outer islands of Green and Rattlesnake lock the ice in around the bigger islands. That gives that ice a chance to stay and build."

The ice between islands, on the other hand, is often treacherous. Strong currents flowing through these passages erode the ice from underneath. A similarly dangerous condition occurs in the area of Mouse Island, just off Catawba Island. The many anglers who employ Chrysler's ice fishing service avoid these troublesome spots by flying over to South Bass Island from the mainland.

Early ice also forms west of Catawba Island, covering the bay in front of Port Clinton. As with the ice west of the Bass islands, this ice is more consistent and stays put late into the season (see Map 1). In warm winters, these may be the only areas that afford ice fishing, but they are both excellent. There is plenty of depth around the Bass islands. In the bay, go out until you reach 17 to 19 feet of water.

LATER ICE

Cold winters create more extensive ice. When that occurs, Capt. Dave Demeter hauls shanties for his Double D ice fishing service out from the mainland to deeper water southwest of the Bass islands.

"I like deeper water," says Demeter. "We run from Catawba State Park along a route that swings west and north around the South Passage (which lies between South Bass and Catawba islands). The ice in the Passage isn't as reliable. The same is true of the ice between South Bass

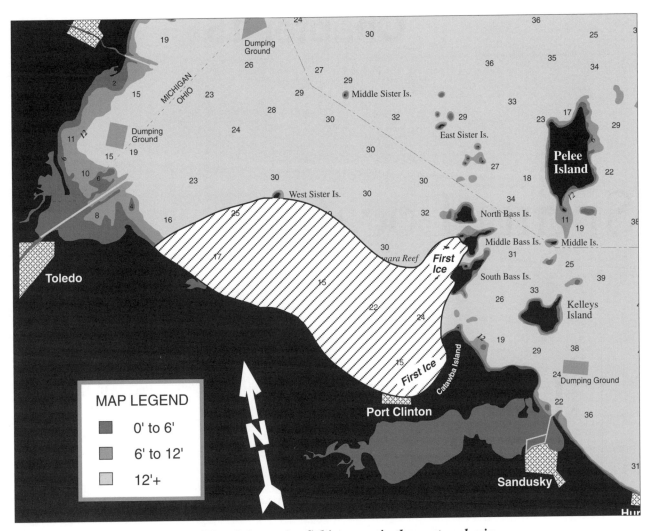

MAP 1: *Primary ice fishing area in the western basin.*

and Kelleys. Most people fish the ice to the west of the islands."

Another popular ice fishing area extends from around Camp Perry to Reno Beach. (Note that the overall ice cap on the lake will be more extensive than is shown on Map 1.) During a hard winter, the ice may reach out as far as West Sister Island, but you shouldn't have to go that far from shore to find walleyes, especially later in the season. The farther you travel from shore, the greater the odds for a mishap with bad ice.

"It takes a pretty cold winter to freeze Lake Erie good," says revered charter captain Jim Fofrich. "The water from Niagara Reef west very seldom freezes prior to the 15th of February. You've got to have a severe winter for that to freeze.

"This is a dynamite area in February and March. And I'm talking about fishing only a half a mile offshore. Those fish are getting ready to spawn. Walleyes weighing 8 to 10 pounds will be right up in 12 to 14 feet of water."

Many anglers venture onto the ice in this area from Crane Creek State Park.

ICE FISHING CHARTERS

Pat Chrysler
P.O. Box 539
Put-In-Bay, OH 43456
(419) 285-4631

Dave Demeter
Double D Ice Fishing Service
P.O. Box 274
Lakeside, OH 43440
(419) 798-9195

Lenny Banyak
1911 South Church Rd.
Marblehead, OH 43440
(419) 734-6155

Chapter 15

Spring Locations

LAKE ERIE'S WALLEYE used to get a reprieve after ice out because few fishermen put boats on the water until mid-April. Not anymore. As soon as the ice breaks up, generally the first week in March, anglers begin taking heavyweight walleyes from open water in the western basin.

ICE OUT

The primary tactic at this time is to vertically jig spoons, vibrating blades and jigs tipped with minnows from boats that are anchored or drifting very slowly. It's similar to the vertical jigging methods used when ice fishing.

"The fish are staging in huge numbers in deeper water," says Capt. Dave Demeter, who operates Double D charters. "They've migrated to this area and they're getting ready to spawn on reefs and run up the Sandusky and Maumee rivers. The very first place I catch them in the spring is all around the Catawba Island and Mouse Island area, throughout the South Passage and out to the mouth of Sandusky Bay (see Map 2)."

Mike Beidel of Fayetteville, Pennsylvania, can vouch for the fishing in this portion of the lake. On March 24, 1995, he caught a 15.95-pound walleye near the mouth of Sandusky Bay. The fish set a new Ohio state record.

To the west of Catawba Island, ice-out walleyes are taken mainly in depths ranging from 22 to 30 feet. The fish hold within striking range of reefs and shorelines all the way from Catawba

Island to the mouth of Maumee Bay and as far out into the lake as West Sister Island.

"They won't start moving shallow until the water warms," says Capt. Jim Fofrich. "That takes place anywhere from the third week in March to the first week in April."

Veteran walleye pro Al Lesh of Warren, Michigan, claims that the Michigan section of Lake Erie also yields walleyes beginning in March. He finds them from Toledo all the way to the mouth of the Detroit River.

"There's a tremendous amount of fish movement between Maumee Bay and the Detroit River," says Lesh.

Few anglers fish east of Sandusky Bay during the walleye's pre-spawn phase, but walleyes do stage 30 to 40 feet deep from Huron to Avon Point in the Ohio portion of the central basin. The bottom here drops off faster than in the western basin, so you need to go out from shore only

---

BEWARE OF ICE FLOWS

When the ice first breaks up, consider waiting until some of the ice flows move off before launching a boat. Many chunks are large enough to be a hazard.

"It's standard," says Michigan walleye expert Al Lesh, "to carry 16-foot two by fours with you to push the ice flows away. Sometimes it's a little bit hairy."

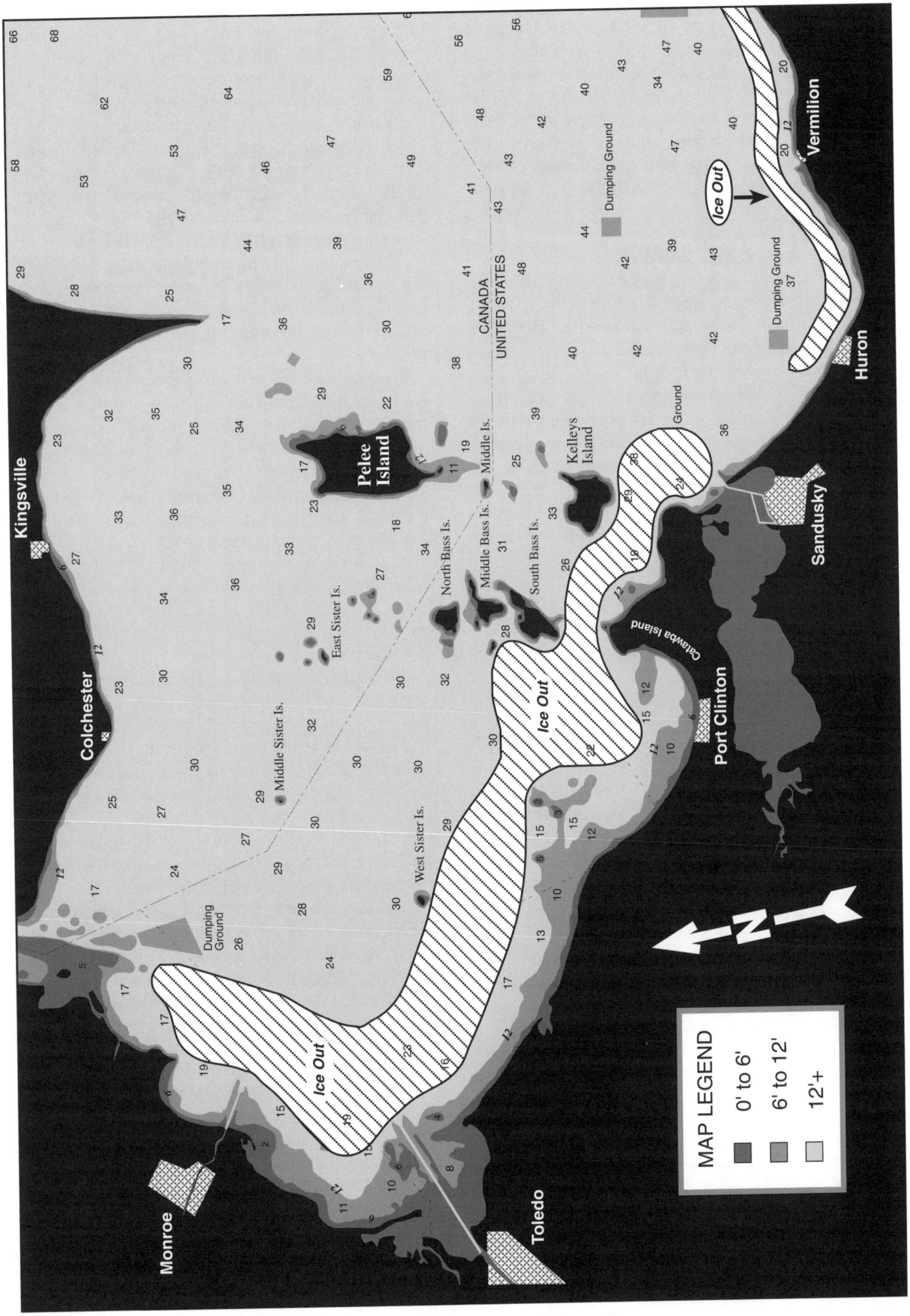

MAP 2: *Ice out.*

1 1/2 to 2 miles. Similar opportunities may exist in other regions of Lake Erie, but they go untested.

"You're not going to catch a lot of fish early here," says Capt. Eddy Able, who docks at Spitzer Lakeside Marina in Lorain, Ohio. "But we've got a fairly good resident population of walleyes. The water warms slower than in the western basin. When their fish are spawning, our fish are just thinking about it."

THE SPAWN

The spawning exodus begins in late March or early April and spans a period of two to three weeks. Not all walleyes spawn at the same time. They continually move in and out of hard-bottom areas where water currents whisk their eggs clean of silt.

About 10 percent of the walleyes run up the Maumee and Sandusky rivers. The rest spawn on the expansive reefs and near shore areas in the western basin that provide capable spawning grounds (see Map 3).

"The reefs west of Catawba Island are excellent at this time," says Capt. Demeter, "such as Niagara, Crib, Toussaint, Cone and Round."

Before the zebra mussel invasion, only the shallowest reefs attracted spawning walleyes. Now the fish find suitable conditions in deeper water.

"By virtue of the zebra mussels," says Capt. Fofrich, "a lot of our deep-water reefs have become viable spawning grounds. Instead of having to have 3 to 5 feet of water for spawning, now walleyes spawn as deep as 16 feet."

Zebra mussels also have enhanced shoreline spawning areas. Masses of walleye move near shore all around Catawba Island and on east past Marblehead. To the west, they move up off beaches between Port Clinton and Maumee Bay. Walleyes also gather on dredgings in Maumee Bay along the edge of the shipping channel. Zebra mussels flourish on these humps and afford a firm bottom, which further increases the walleye's spawning habitat.

The productive depth near shore varies from 3 to 17 feet. When storms stir up silt from the bottom and flush a muddy flow out of the Maumee River, water visibility along the southern shoreline of the western basin may be reduced to inches. The rule of thumb is to fish shallow in dirty water and deep in clear water.

"Males weighing up to 5 pounds can be caught readily on the reefs," says Demeter. "You don't catch many big females on top of the reefs, but you do get them on the beaches and inshore rock piles. Why? I don't know."

Casting jigs tipped with minnows is by far the most popular tactic for fishing reefs and near shore. Dragging spinner rigs with bottom bouncers and slow-trolling long minnow crankbaits are productive, too, during this period.

The bank stretching from Huron to Avon Point in the central basin attracts spawning walleyes during the latter part of April and early May (see Map 3). The fish move up on rocky bottoms in 6 to 25 feet of water. When Capt. Able leaves his dock at Spitzer Lakeside Marina in Lorain, Ohio, a short boat ride puts him over good numbers of fish.

"When they're on the beach," says Able, "you mainly catch them fishing dead on the bottom. I get up in the rocks and fish them hard with jigs tipped with crawlers or minnows and weight-forward spinners."

The water tends to be clearer here than in the western basin, which can make walleyes more wary. Able finds the shallow fishing better after a heavy rainfall has stained the water.

"You don't want it to look like chocolate milk," says Able, "but they'll usually stay shallow longer if the water has a mossy green color to it."

This doesn't mean that you can't take walleyes in clear, shallow water. Able's clients have made excellent catches less than 12 feet deep in water so transparent he could see the white bellies of walleyes when they rolled to take jigs. The fish are shallowest early in the morning and gradually back out to deeper water as the day brightens.

PRE- & POST-SPAWN WALLEYES

While the Ohio portion of the western basin attracts the most attention from anglers during the spawn, Capt. Lesh also fares well fishing near the Michigan shoreline at this time (see Map 3).

"You can work sand and gravel beaches in early spring from Maumee Bay to the Detroit River. Some spots are better than others. They're migrating, going back and forth. Sometimes they move up to 5 feet of water on flats."

CAMP PERRY FIRING RANGE

Many of the major spawning reefs in the western basin fall within the Camp Perry firing range. The boundaries for this danger zone are show on Marine Navigational Chart #14830 and are also marked with orange and white buoys bearing the words "Range Impact Area."

Firing in this area is normally conducted between 8 a.m. and 5 p.m. Monday through Friday except federal holidays. The size of the impact area may vary from year to year. For more information, contact the Camp Perry Range Safety Office on marine VHF channel 16, or telephone (419) 635-4103 for specific firing schedules.

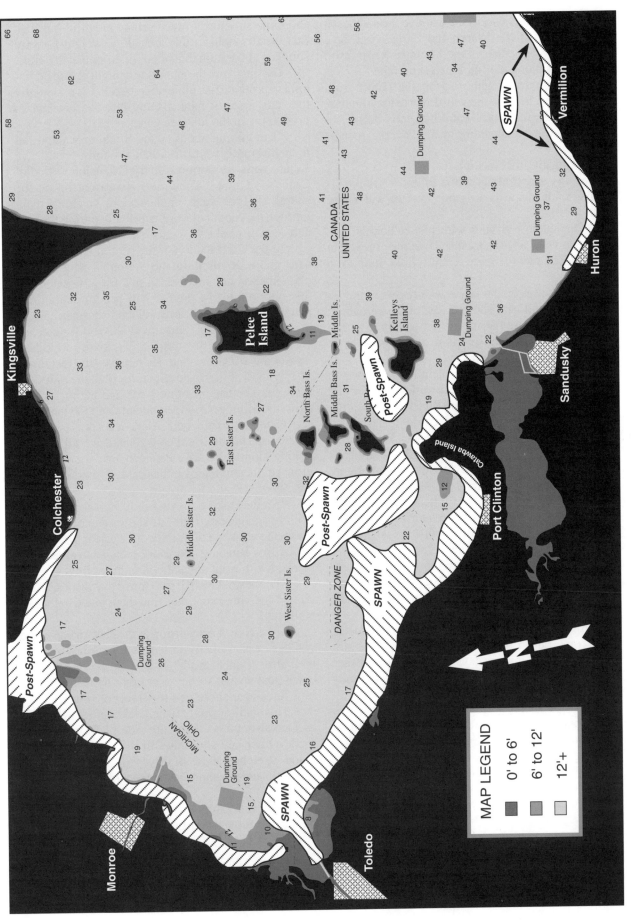

MAP 3: *Spawn and post-spawn.*

Lesh believes many of the walleyes he catches in shallow water in late March and Early April have already spawned, either in the Maumee River or on shallow flats along the Michigan shoreline.

"The fish really gang up on the banks from Monroe (Brest Bay) all the way down to the Maumee River," says Lesh. "You'll catch big, early fish in 5 to 10 feet of water depending on the weather conditions."

During this brief feeding spree, Lesh scores well casting jigs and trolling subtle minnow crankbaits behind small planer boards in 5 feet of water (see Chapter 10).

"The shallow fishing with planer boards lasts about two weeks," says Lesh. "Then they move out into 14 to 18 feet of water. They'll hold there for a month."

While some of the walleyes are spawning on Ohio's reefs and near shore areas, others remain in deeper water. These fish are either waiting to spawn or have already spawned. If you're after big walleyes, this is where you should fish.

"The spawning period generally takes two to three weeks," says professional walleye angler and former Lake Erie charter captain Rick LaCourse. "It's a gradual movement. Some fish come in and spawn and move back out to deeper water. I've caught bunches of big, post-spawn females trolling crankbaits in 38 feet of water when the surface water temperature was only 40 degrees."

One of the better places for heavyweight, post-spawn walleyes is an area stretching north from Niagara reef to northwest of North Bass Island (see map 3). Many charter captains believe the walleyes that gang up northwest of North Bass actually spawn on the islands. Another key area for post-spawn walleyes lies between Kelleys Island and Middle Bass Island.

"After they finish spawning," says Capt. Demeter, "they come out to these deep-water areas and stay near the bottom for a few days. The best method then is something that moves very slowly, a jig and minnow combination or a spoon and minnow."

Once the walleyes recuperate, they move higher off the bottom and begin feeding in earnest. This is when slow-trolling crankbaits behind small boards and dragging spinner rigs behind bottom bouncers can produced phenomenal catches of big fish. As the fish become more active and suspend 8 to 10 feet above bottom, weight-forward spinners also come into play.

From Huron to Avon Point in the central basin, post-spawn walleyes tend to move in and out of shoreline structure to feed on the plentiful bait fish that usually hold in this area. Jigs, weight-forward spinners and bottom bouncers all do well at this time.

Casting from the shoreline at night is also beginning to produce fish along this stretch. It's essentially the same type of bank fishing that has become so productive in the fall (see Chapter 13).

"I'm talking about taking limits of walleyes at night that rarely weigh less than 4 pounds," says Dave Kelch, with the Lorain County Extension Office of Ohio Sea Grant. "They push shad right up on the shoreline. Last year, anglers were catching them through the month of May, especially during the first and second weeks."

In the Ohio section of the central basin, fishing near shore at night in the spring is such a new phenomenon that no one can say just how extensive this opportunity is, or if it will become an annual pattern. Frank Scalish, an excellent fisherman and the talented artist who illustrated this book, catches walleyes in May by casting crankbaits to riprap breakwalls off Cleveland. He believes the fast drop-offs by these man-made structures hold the fish. The same may be true of other ports and harbors to the east, including Fairport, Ashtabula and Conneaut.

Charter captain Pete Alex, who docks at Erie Angler Marina in Erie, Pennsylvania, says that night fishing along the entire Pennsylvania shoreline has grown quite popular over the past five years (see Map 5 & 6).

"Anglers take walleyes in 2 to 12 feet of water by trolling and casting right off shore. The better areas are on the west end of the city of Erie near the mouths of Godfrey Run and Crooked Creek. Both creeks are stocked with trout and salmon in the spring.

"Those stocked fish run from 6 to 9 inches," says Alex, "and you sometimes find them in the bellies of walleyes."

In the New York portion of the eastern basin, the walleye season opens on the first Saturday in May, well after resident walleyes have spawned. Anglers catch post-spawn walleyes at night by trolling minnow lures near shore in 4 to 10 feet of water.

This shallow, night fishery takes place as far east as Lackawanna on the south side of Buffalo, New York. Other key shorelines in the eastern basin include stretches west of Sturgeon Point, west of Dunkirk, and the shoreline in front of Barcelona (see Map 6).

There are no reports of similar near-shore fishing on the Canadian side of the lake.

Chapter 16

Late Spring & Summer Locations

Once the walleyes recover from spawning, their entire existence centers on feeding. Through the latter part of May and the month of June, walleyes in the western basin spend most of their time feeding in open water. This is the traditional time for slinging weight-forward spinners, especially in murky water or when it's windy or cloudy.

"Conditions that reduce light penetration in the western basin favor weight-forward spinners," says Capt. Demeter. "Back when the water was dirty, we used to look for clear water. Now we look for stained water."

In clear water, weighted spinner rigs and the various trolling methods described in the previous chapters often catch more fish than weight-forward spinners.

Because walleyes constantly roam the open expanses of Lake Erie following bait fish, it's impossible to predict exactly where they will be at any given time. Although their movements may vary from one year to the next, they do follow fairly consistent seasonal patterns that strongly suggest where you should begin searching for them.

THE WESTERN BASIN

From about mid-May to mid-June, good numbers of walleyes stay within an area of the western basin encompassed by West Sister Island, Niagara Reef, the Bass islands and East Sister Island (see Map 4).

The well known Sister Island Triangle, formed by Middle Sister, East Sister and West Sister, sometimes holds fish throughout the summer (see Map 4).

"Generally," says Capt. Demeter, "from mid to late June you should be able to catch fish anywhere in that triangle."

The range of the walleye in the island area expands in July to include the east sides of Kelleys and Pelee islands (see Map 4).

The extreme west end of Lake Erie consistently holds fish from mid-May to the end of July. Capt. Jerry Lee, of Livonia, Michigan, has netted countless limits of walleyes from this area over the past 18 years. He usually starts out in May fishing the southern end of the lake in front of Maumee Bay. As the water warms, he moves north with the fish and concentrates more in the area of Brest Bay. His primary tactic is trolling crankbaits behind big boards.

"The fish hold in this area," says Lee, "until the water temperature hits 80 degrees. Then they move east to deeper water."

The Canadian side of Erie remains relatively untapped by anglers because the brunt of the fishing pressure comes from the American side. Throughout much of the season, walleyes are so abundant in U.S. waters there is no need to venture into Canada. Walleyes, however, are plentiful north of the boarder. You need only look into the nets of Canadian commercial fishermen to verify this fact.

Capt. Joe Belanger, who runs charters out of Leamington, Ontario, early in the season, finds plenty of fish for his clients from the Detroit River to Pelee Point from mid-May through June.

"Most of the time," says Belanger, "I find them close in 20 to 22 feet of water (see Map 4)."

When Capt. Dave Demeter has trouble finding fish in the island area in July, he often ventures north across the western basin and gets into them in the deep water south of Colchester, Ontario.

"One reason I go to Canada," says Demeter, "is to get away from all the boats. In the clear water we have today, heavy traffic makes the fish tougher to catch."

THE WALLEYE MIGRATION

Probably more than half of the walleye population frequents the western basin all year, but a substantial portion of the fish travels widely. To learn more about these movements, fisheries biologists have tagged more than 30,000 walleyes over the past 10 years as part of an interagency study that involves Ontario, Michigan, Ohio, Pennsylvania and New York. The study strongly indicates that Lake Erie's walleyes are comprised of several different stocks of fish.

"The Maumee stock spawns in the Maumee River," says Roger Knight, who Supervises the Lake Erie Research Station for the Ohio Department of Natural Resources. "After spawning, some of these fish go up through the Detroit River as far north as Lake Huron. The rest stay in the western basin.

"The Sandusky River stock goes east. They're not doing as well because of a dam on the river that prevents them from reaching prime spawning habitat. The Grand River stock appears to be different from either one of those.

"There is a reef spawning stock, or different stocks of reef spawners. We've always thought that they were contributing most of the hatch to the lake. That may change over time. There's a lot we don't know."

The study of genetics in Lake Erie walleye may help fisheries biologists confirm the existence of individual stocks and teach us more about their habits. In the future, Lake Erie's walleyes may be managed on a stock-by-stock basis, with a variety of regulations geared to different zones of the lake. At this point, the tagging studies have revealed general seasonal patterns of walleye movements.

"After they spawn in the western basin," says Knight, "a group of large females moves east and spends the entire summer in the central basin. Some of them go as far as the eastern basin, clear down off of Dunkirk, New York."

The walleyes that migrate east typically run 3 to 8 pounds or more. If you dream of filling a cooler with heavyweight walleyes, head for the central and eastern basins in the summertime and employ big-water trolling tactics. Walleyes in the western basin run 1 to 4 pounds in the summer with an occasional trophy fish. Trolling and casting methods score there, depending on the weather and water conditions.

Data from the tagging study shows that more walleyes move into the eastern basin in some years than in others, and this largely determines how good the fishing will be in a given season. The same may be said of the eastern end of the central basin.

The vastness of the central and eastern basins, the mobility of the walleye and the ever-changing nature of the lake makes finding the fish a considerable challenge. They could be virtually anywhere. This is where a good sonar and a Loran or GPS unit is indispensable (see Chapter 2).

THE CENTRAL BASIN

By mid-May, walleyes are spilling out of the western basin on the Ohio side of the lake. The span of water from Sandusky to Lorain holds fish throughout the summer (see Map 4).

"From about the 15th of May to the third week of June," says Capt. Jim Fofrich, "this is some of the best fishing on the lake. Many big fish hold close to shore in 26 to 34 feet of water."

A prime walleye structure in this area is the west side of a sand bar that extends from Lorain north to the Canadian line (see Map 4).

"It's a natural barrier," says pro walleye angler Rick LaCourse. The bar rises from 48 feet to 32 feet and then drops off into the deeper part of the central basin east of Lorain.

"Walleyes push bait fish against that bar and feed on them. Once the walleyes pass over the bar, they may roam as far as the eastern basin."

In May and June, Capt. Eddy Able, who docks at Spitzer Lakeside Marina in Lorain, Ohio, often finds walleyes within 4 miles of the mainland. His clients do well casting weight-forward spinners.

"As the summer progresses and the walleyes move deeper," says Able, "I run northeast of the sandbar 12 to 20 miles. We still take some walleyes casting, but trolling is more productive."

Capt. Andy Emrisko, who runs charters out of Cleveland Lakefront State Park, begins catching walleyes in this section of the central basin in mid-May. The fishing steadily improves as the water warms and more walleyes migrate east from the western basin.

"The magic water temperature," says Emrisko, "is 55 degrees. Everything starts biting here about that time, and it gets better as the water warms up."

120

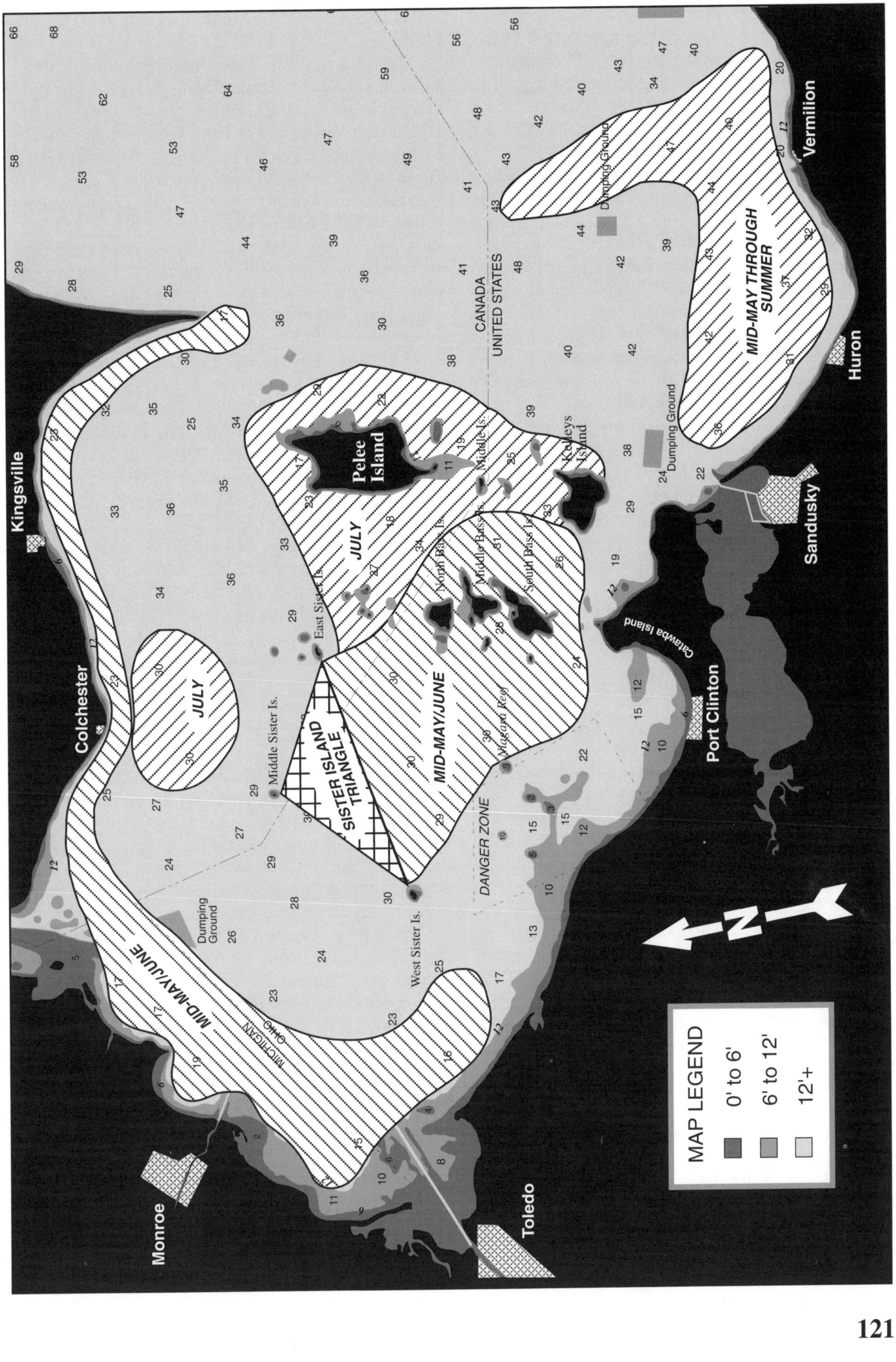

MAP 4: *The western basin.*

MAP LEGEND

0' to 6'

6' to 12'

12'+

Emrisko uses water temperature as a general guide to determine where to begin trolling for walleyes. When the water temperature is 55 degrees, he runs out from the mainland and begins fishing where the bottom depth drops to 55 feet. When the water warms to 60 degrees, he starts in 60 feet of water, and so on (see Map 5).

"Their movement deeper seems to be a lot faster now that the water is clearer," says Emrisko. "In August, I may be 27 miles out over 80 feet of water."

By late summer, Ron Johnson, a champion walleye angler who runs charters out of Fairport Harbor, also makes long runs to reach deep water. In recent years he has been running northwest.

"In this part of the lake," says Johnson, "there is a hole off of Cleveland that's about 80 feet deep, which is a few feet deeper than the rest of the lake. For some reason it's there, and it holds fish."

As with Emrisko, Johnson trolls closer to the mainland in the spring and works deeper as the water warms. He starts in May trolling Hot 'N' Tots on flat lines within 4 miles of the shoreline. By June, he's running 5 to 13 miles out and usually to the west of Fairport Harbor. Here, he finds more structure and faster depth changes, such as the sand bar off Mentor Harbor.

"It drops from 32 feet to about 42 feet," says Johnson. "Then there's a little trough and it comes back up to about 38. It drops to 60-foot on out from there. The bar generally always has some fish, and it's real good in the spring.

"There's also structure off of Euclid General Hospital. It comes in just a little bit east of the Eastlake power plant. It's a little point of rock and clay and it holds fish in the spring."

Walleyes do remain near shore during the summer in the central basin, but they tend to run smaller and are less abundant than those that stay out in deeper water.

"In the last year or two," says Kevin Kayle, supervisor of the Lake Erie Research Station in Fairport, "we've noticed that there is a fishery of smaller walleye within the first 2 to 4 miles of the shoreline. They run from 15 to 24 inches and usually frequent a depth range from 35 to 55 feet."

Art Lyon, a noted walleye angler from Conneaut, Ohio, often takes advantage of this near-shore fishery when he heads out from Conneaut Harbor, especially early in the summer. For bigger fish, however, he recommends fishing well offshore during July, August and September.

"A lot of charter boats now," says Lyon, "head out close to the Canadian line and fish water more than 70 feet deep. When they catch them before 10 a.m., the fish may be suspended 35 to 40 feet deep. Later in the day, you'll get them a little deeper,

probably around 50 feet. Sometimes they're 60 feet or deeper."

Trolling for deep-water walleyes in the central basin along Pennsylvania begins in late May and June. This is when Capt. Pete Alex, who charters out of Erie Angler Marina in Erie, Pennsylvania, takes walleye by trolling closer to shore 52 to 65 feet deep. These likely are resident fish (see Maps 5 & 6).

The action with big walleyes in the Pennsylvania portion of Lake Erie picks up around the end of June with the arrival of fish that have migrated from the western basin. Alex first finds them in 55 to 70 feet of water. As the water warms through July and into August, he follows the fish as they progressively move out over 120 feet of water (see Maps 5 & 6).

"We have two notable structures within 7 miles of our port," says Alex. "The one to the west is called the Trenches. The one to the east we call the Mountain. In mid-August," says Alex, "the walleyes begin migrating to shallower water. They feed heavily and move south and west. Most of them have left Pennsylvania waters by the end of September (see Maps 5 & 6)."

Regardless of the bottom depth, Alex consistently takes suspended walleyes by trolling crankbaits with big boards and diving planes in the upper 25 feet of water and also in the 35- to 40-foot range.

Walleye movements on the Canadian side of the central basin mimic what takes place on the U.S. side. The sportfishing pressure isn't nearly as intense in Canada, but the commercial fishing industry harvests enormous quantities of walleyes from the central basin.

Walleyes on the Canadian side of the lake usually follow the northern shoreline east around Pelee Point into the central basin. A few fish begin showing up in Erieau in early June. By the latter part of June, the fishing reaches full swing in Erieau and farther east to Port Glasgow. The walleyes typically light up Port Stanley and waters farther east early in July.

Following the walleye migration, Capt. Joe Belanger moves his operation in June from Leamington, Ontario, in the western basin to Erieau in the central basin. He takes most of his fish trolling there with big boards and downriggers.

"Early in June," says Belanger, "we catch them close to shore in 30 to 45 feet of water. Then the water warms up and the fish move out. In mid-July and August, we may be fishing over 65 to 80 feet of water.

"It depends on the weather and what the bait fish are doing. In some years, I rarely have to go out as far as 10 miles to find them. Then there are times when I have to go 20 miles out near the U.S. border. Those fish will swim 5 to 10 miles in one night."

Art Grayling, who runs charters out of Glasgow, Ontario, has fished the central basin for 40 years both

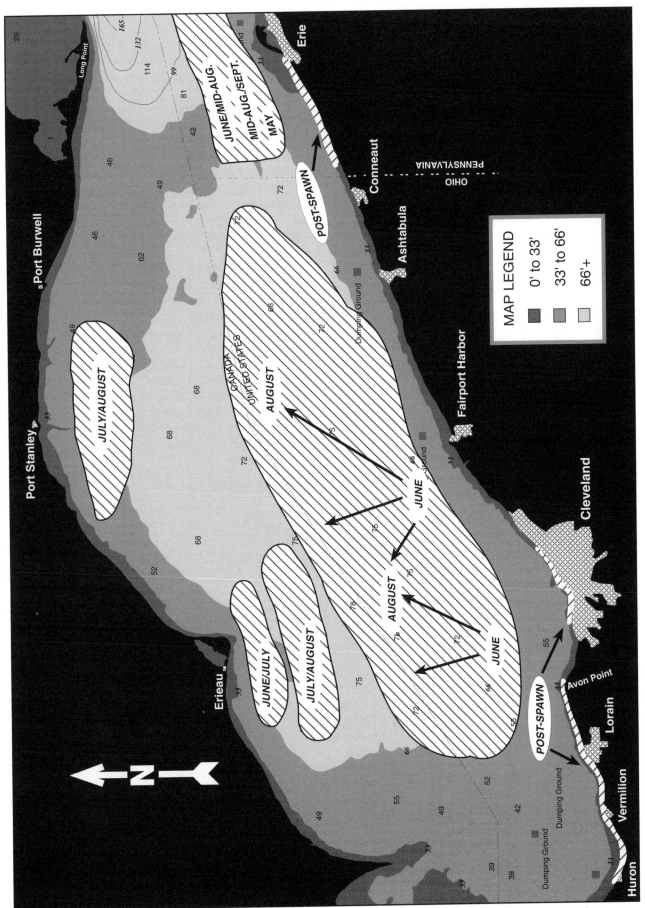

MAP 5: *The central basin.*

as a commercial fisherman and, for the past 20 years, as a charter captain. He calls 65 feet the magic depth for this part of the central basin, because it marks the edge of a rocky bottom.

"You can get 65 feet of water about 10 miles out from Port Stanley," he says. "From Glasgow you need to go out about 5 miles. It's all rock inside of that and the walleyes just seem to hang around that edge."

In recent years, Grayling has begun taking his clients southwest past Erieau later in the summer. He does so to escape the flotilla of commercial fishermen who dredge the bottom in the Port Glasgow and Port Stanley area for smelt, a primary forage for walleyes in the central basin. The trawlers, claims Grayling, rip up the bottom, remove the forage, and push the walleyes out of the area.

THE EASTERN BASIN

As with the central basin, resident walleyes in the eastern basin provide fishing opportunities early in the season. But the midsummer, trolling fishery that occurs well offshore is comprised mainly of walleyes that have migrated from the west.

"We believe the walleyes taken here in the spring are local fish," says Don Einhouse, senior aquatic biologist for New York State's Department of Environmental Conservation. "Immediately following the spawn, a fishery develops along the 50- to 60-foot contour. That usually happens in the early part of June. By the end of June through August, most of the better fishing is between the 75- and 100-foot contour (see Map 6).

"I think of the walleye population as a gradient from west to east. The further west you go on Lake Erie, the more walleyes there are. The eastern basin isn't as productive because it's clearer and more oligotrophic. But by our standards, the walleye fishing has been pretty darn good."

Capt. Bill King, who runs charters out of Chadwick Bay Marina in Dunkirk Harbor, New York, agrees. He claims that the walleyes seem to bite better later in the year than in the past, with the end of July, August and September being especially productive in the eastern basin. At times he catches walleyes 60 to 80 feet down over water 120 feet deep. Good fishing continues until about mid-October.

"In October," says King, "we also take steelhead, salmon and late trout."

The Canadian side of the eastern basin produces walleyes in July and August, and it receives less fishing pressure than other parts of the lake. Catches have been reported between Nanticoke and Hoover Point, and to the east and west of Port Colborne (see Map 6).

ARTIFICIAL REEFS

To help attract fish for anglers, artificial reefs, made from scrap rock and concrete, were constructed near Lorain and Lakewood, Ohio. They lie in 28 to 30 feet of water and attract a wide variety of fish, including walleyes.

The Lorain reef, now called the Polish Fisherman's Artificial Reef, is composed of two reefs measuring 1,400 by 700 feet in length. The reefs are marked by buoys. The larger reef is a mile east of Lorain harbor and about three-quarters of a mile offshore, directly in front of McDonald's golden arches. The smaller reef lies approximately 100 yards north of the middle buoy.

The Lakewood reef, renamed the Cuyahoga County Commissioners Reef, measures 800 feet. A series of 300-foot reefs may be found nearby. You'll find these structures just east of Lakewood Park, about half of a mile offshore. Look for a water pipe coming out of the cliff.

For more information on the reefs and how to find them, contact Ohio Sea Grant, Lorain County Extension Office, 42110 Russia Rd., Elyria, OH 44035. Phone: (216) 322-0127.

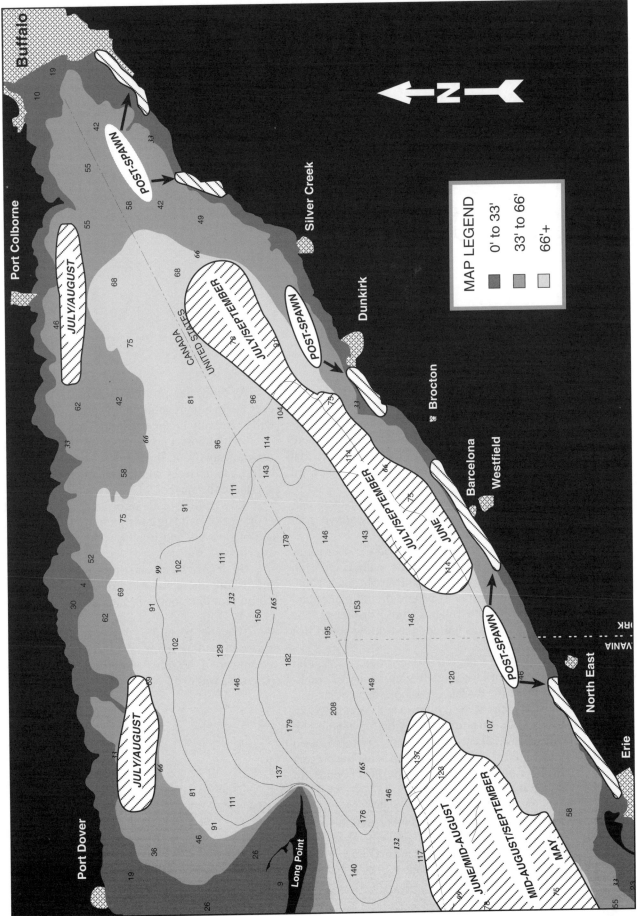

MAP 6: *The eastern basin.*

125

Chapter 17

Fall Locations

FISHING TAILS off in the eastern and central basins in September and October, but the action starts picking up again in the western basin. By October, walleyes are feeding more actively in the western basin and it appears that they are already returning from their eastward migration.

From mid-September through November, casting and trolling methods yield walleye from Huron to Niagara Reef (see Map 7).

A few years ago, I spent an October afternoon fishing north of Huron with Capt. Bob Troxel and my good Friend Bob Mrugacz. Capt. Troxel set out spoons behind diving planes and ran them at depths ranging from 30 to 40 feet. The key that day was holding the trolling speed just under 2 m.p.h.

Walleyes engulfed our spoons at regular intervals until we actually grew weary of cranking them in. By late afternoon, our cooler was stuffed with fish weighing up to 8 pounds. When we got our last bite of the day before heading in, Mrugacz and I encouraged Capt. Troxel to take a turn landing a fish. It wound up being the biggest walleye of the day, an ounce shy of 12 pounds. So much for being nice guys.

Fishing from the bank at night starts producing heavy walleyes in November, and the action continues right on through December along Lorain, Huron, Catawba Island in Ohio, and Luna Pier in Michigan (see Chapter 13).

As the water cools in December, the walleyes begin congregating in the areas where they will eventually be taken through the ice.

"It's almost a pre-staging for the spawning season," says Capt. Jim Fofrich. "You catch them before ice-up right where you catch them after ice-out in the spring."

Slow trolling methods produce at the tail end of the season as do jig and minnow combinations, and blade baits and jigging spoons tipped with minnows.

On the Michigan end of the lake, pro angler and fishing instructor Al Lesh often fishes until ice-up near the mouth of Maumee Bay (see Map 7).

"Weather permitting," says Lesh, "I always try to go fishing there on my birthday. That's December 14. My idea of a birthday present is a 10-pound walleye."

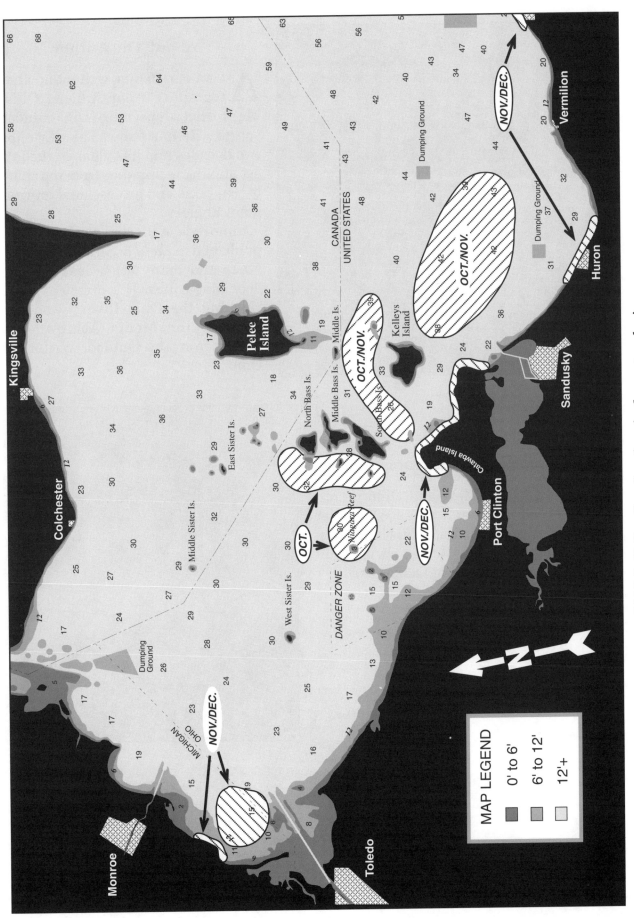

MAP 7: *Fall walleye locations in the western basin.*

About The Author

A N AWARD WINNING writer and photographer from Athens, Ohio, Mark Hicks specializes in outdoor sports. He has fished Lake Erie for two decades and has gleaned the latest angling techniques from top charter captains and professional tournament anglers.

Hundreds of his articles have been published in *Field & Stream, Fishing Facts* and many other leading outdoor magazines. His previous book, "Fishing the Ohio River," won the Outstanding Media Achievement Award from the Outdoor Writers of Ohio.

About The Illustrator

F RANK SCALISH of Cleveland, Ohio, is both a talented artist and an expert angler who has proven his fishing skills in tournaments. His detailed drawings perfectly illustrate successful fishing techniques.

His business address is:
263 East 149th St.
Cleveland, OH 44110.
(216) 623-1616.

Additional copies of *Lake Erie Walleye* may be ordered through the mail.

Send $14.95 plus $3 shipping.
(Ohio residents add $0.93 tax)

BIG RIVER PRESS
P.O. Box 130
Millfield, OH 45761

CAUTION
The author may not be held responsible for any mishaps that may occur while fishing Lake Erie. Always use good common sense when visiting this waterway and heed small craft warnings.